# Understanding AI and ML in Modern Security: A Comprehensive Guide from Beginners to Advanced Practitioners

**Rajashekhar Reddy Kethireddy**
Software Architecture and DevOps

© 2024

# Authors

## Rajashekhar Reddy Kethireddy

Rajashekhar Reddy Kethireddy is a seasoned expert in software architecture and DevOps, boasting over a decade of experience in enterprise-level security engineering and automation. His career began after earning a Bachelor's degree in Engineering from Jawaharlal Nehru Technological University, Hyderabad, in 2012, followed by a Master's in Electrical Engineering from Cleveland State University in 2015.

Since then, Rajashekhar has held pivotal roles at prominent companies like IBM, where he has worked since 2019, first as a Senior DevOps Engineer and later as a Software Architect. In his current role at IBM (May 2023 – present), he focuses on developing highly reliable and scalable cloud storage solutions within IBM Cloud. He also plays a key role in SOC2, HITRUST, GDPR, and HIPAA compliance initiatives, ensuring the services meet stringent security and privacy standards.

Rajashekhar's work includes implementing continuous integration (CI) and continuous deployment (CD) pipelines, leveraging tools like Ansible, Jenkins, and Kubernetes to automate cloud infrastructure management. His leadership extends to overseeing complex cloud storage enhancements and driving innovation across teams to optimize performance, reduce downtime, and enhance security protocols.

Earlier in his career, Rajashekhar contributed to various projects, such as leading efforts to integrate Cleversafe into IBM's public cloud offerings, supporting object storage, automating AWS components, and enhancing monitoring systems with tools like New Relic, ELK, and Grafana. His hands-on approach and deep technical knowledge in cloud infrastructure, security standards, and automation have made him a highly respected figure in the industry.

Rajashekhar is not only an expert in technical execution but also a strong leader in agile, fast-paced environments. His ability to collaborate with cross-functional teams and improve operational efficiency makes him a key figure in cloud infrastructure and DevOps.

# Reviewers

## Shrey Modi

Shrey Modi is an innovator and change-maker dedicated to making a significant impact on people's lives through machine learning. With experience working on groundbreaking projects at ISRO, Shrey has a deep understanding of how technology can drive change. He founded the first AI Research Club across 23 California State University campuses, creating a vibrant community for AI enthusiasts and researchers. As a member of the AI steering committee at CSULB, he played a pivotal role in guiding the direction of AI initiatives. Shrey is also the author of a book on machine learning, aimed at making the field accessible to beginners and those eager to explore AI. His research accomplishments include publishing 8 papers that have garnered over 120 citations, highlighting his dedication to advancing the field. Shrey's mission is to continue leveraging AI to develop innovative solutions that inspire others and contribute to the transformative power of technology.

## Dinesh Reddy Chittibala

Dinesh brings over a decade of expertise in DevSecOps, where I focus on embedding security at every stage of the development and operations lifecycle. My experience spans cloud infrastructure, automation, and security protocols, ensuring robust, scalable, and secure systems. For the past four years, I've also specialized in MLOps, overseeing the secure deployment, management, and monitoring of machine learning models in production environments.

I've worked extensively with AWS security tools, including advanced configurations in AWS WAF for Content Security Policy (CSP) enforcement, enhancing web application protection. As a passionate developer, Golang is my language of choice, valued for its efficiency and performance in building high-availability systems. My commitment to optimizing the intersection of security, operations, and machine learning has helped drive secure, scalable solutions across various platforms.

# Preface

Welcome to a journey into the heart of cybersecurity powered by artificial intelligence and machine learning—fields that are rapidly reshaping the landscape of digital defense and offense. This book is born from a profound need to demystify the complexities of AI and ML, especially in how they intersect with our needs for safety and privacy in an increasingly interconnected world. As you turn these pages, you'll discover insights drawn from the latest research, expert interviews, and frontline experiences in applying AI to real-world security challenges.

My/Our inspiration for writing this guide stems from witnessing the rapid advancements in technology and the parallel challenges these pose to security professionals, developers, and policymakers. The double-edged sword of AI and ML technologies offers unprecedented opportunities to enhance security measures but also presents sophisticated tools for adversaries. This book is not just an academic exploration; it's a call to better understand and harness these technologies to create a safer digital future. Through the concepts and case studies discussed here, my hope is to empower you with knowledge and inspire you to engage in the ethical development and deployment of AI in security roles.

## What to Expect

This book serves as a comprehensive guide for anyone interested in understanding and leveraging AI and ML in security, whether you're a beginner exploring the basics or a professional seeking to enhance your expertise. It starts by laying a strong foundation with the core principles, concepts, and methodologies of AI and ML, essential for understanding more advanced topics later on. You'll delve into real-world applications through detailed case studies, gaining insights into how these technologies are currently being used in the security field, including both successful strategies and common pitfalls. Practical, hands-on guides are included to help you integrate AI tools into your own security frameworks, from setting up AI-driven threat detection systems to automating incident responses, ensuring that the content is not just theoretical but actionable. For those eager to explore further, advanced chapters cover cutting-edge applications like AI in encryption, predictive security models, and the threats posed by adversarial AI, pushing the boundaries of what is possible in AI-powered security. The book also addresses the ethical and legal considerations of deploying AI in security, a critical component for ensuring responsible use of these technologies. Finally, it looks ahead to future trends, such as quantum computing and AI's role in global security governance, preparing you for the next generation of challenges and innovations. Each chapter builds on the previous one, creating a cohesive narrative that educates and engages. By the end, you'll not only understand how AI and ML can enhance security but also be equipped to implement these technologies ethically and effectively. This book is designed to transform curiosity into expertise, opening new possibilities in the realm of digital security with every page.

# Contents

| | |
|---|---|
| Authors | iii |
| Reviewers | v |
| Preface | vii |
| Foreword | xiii |

## I Introduction — 1

**1 Understanding Artificial Intelligence and Machine Learning — 3**
- 1.1 What is Machine Learning? — 3
- 1.2 How AI and ML Differ from Traditional Computing — 4
- 1.3 Real-World Applications of AI and ML in Security — 4
- 1.4 Engaging with the Concepts — 7
  - 1.4.1 Ethical Use of AI in Surveillance — 7
  - 1.4.2 Bias in Machine Learning Models — 7
  - 1.4.3 AI in Threat Detection and Response — 8
  - 1.4.4 Sustainable AI Deployment — 8
- 1.5 Learnings? — 8

**2 Foundational Technologies — 11**
- 2.1 What Will We Learn? — 11
- 2.2 What Are These ML Algorithms — 12
- 2.3 Neural Networks and Deep Learning in Security — 13
- 2.4 Data Processing and Analysing Techniques — 14
- 2.5 Discussion — 15
- 2.6 Learnings? — 16

**3 Fundamentals of Machine Learning — 19**
- 3.1 Implementation Strategies — 19
- 3.2 Integrating AI into Existing Security Frameworks — 20
- 3.3 Building AI-Driven Security Tools — 21
- 3.4 Automating Threat Detection and Response — 22
- 3.5 Discussion — 23
- 3.6 Thinking — 24

## 4 Real Life Case Studies — 25
- 4.1 Introduction — 25
- 4.2 Retail Sector: Preventing Fraud with Machine Learning? — 26
- 4.3 Healthcare: Protecting Sensitive Data through AI — 27
- 4.4 Government: National Security Enhancements with AI — 28
- 4.5 AI Failures in Security — 29
- 4.6 Discussion — 31
- 4.7 Learnings — 32

## 5 Advanced Topics — 33
- 5.1 Introduction — 33
- 5.2 Predictive Security: Anticipating Threats with AI — 34
- 5.3 Adversarial AI: Understanding and Defending Against AI Exploits — 35
- 5.4 AI in Encryption and Cryptography — 36
- 5.5 Discussion — 37
- 5.6 Learnings? — 38

## 6 Ethical and Legal Considerations — 39
- 6.1 Introduction — 39
- 6.2 Balancing Security Needs with Privacy Rights — 40
  - 6.2.1 Discussion Points: — 40
- 6.3 Ethical AI Use in Surveillance and Monitoring — 41
  - 6.3.1 Discussion Points: — 41
- 6.4 Interactive Discussion: Navigating Ethical and Legal Terrain — 42
  - 6.4.1 Discussion Points: — 42
- 6.5 Key Learnings and Reflections — 43

## 7 Regulations and Compliance in AI Security — 45
- 7.1 Introduction — 45
- 7.2 The Growing Importance of AI Regulation — 46
  - 7.2.1 Key Regulations Affecting AI in Security — 46
    - 7.2.1.1 General Data Protection Regulation (GDPR) — 46
    - 7.2.1.2 California Consumer Privacy Act (CCPA) — 47
    - 7.2.1.3 AI Act (European Union) — 47
    - 7.2.1.4 National AI Initiative Act (United States) — 48
    - 7.2.1.5 Sector-Specific Regulations — 48
- 7.3 Emerging Trends in AI Regulation — 48
- 7.4 Discussion — 50
- 7.5 Learnings? — 50

## 8 AI and IoT Security — 51
- 8.1 Introduction — 51
- 8.2 The Unique Challenges of IoT Security — 52
  - 8.2.1 Diverse and Fragmented Ecosystem — 53
    - 8.2.1.1 Limited Processing Power and Storage — 53

|     |       |                                                      |    |
|-----|-------|------------------------------------------------------|----|
|     | 8.3   | Practical Solutions for Securing IoT with AI         | 55 |
|     | 8.3.1 | Deploy AI-Driven Security Gateways                   | 56 |
|     | 8.3.2 | Use Lightweight AI Models                            | 56 |
|     | 8.3.3 | Adopt Edge AI for Real-Time Security                 | 56 |
|     | 8.3.4 | Implement Continuous Learning and Adaptation         | 56 |
|     | 8.3.5 | Integrate AI with Existing Security Frameworks       | 56 |
|     | 8.4   | Challenges of Implementing AI in IoT Security        | 57 |
|     | 8.4.1 | Data Privacy Concerns                                | 57 |
|     | 8.5   | Learning?                                            | 57 |
| **9** | **Future Trends and Predictions** |                            | **59** |
|     | 9.1   | Introduction and Basic Concepts                      | 59 |
|     | 9.2   | Quantum Computing and AI Security                    | 60 |
|     | 9.2.1 | Discussion Points                                    | 60 |
|     | 9.3   | Preparing for AI-Enhanced Cyberattacks               | 61 |
|     | 9.3.1 | Discussion Points                                    | 61 |
|     | 9.4   | Discussion                                           | 62 |
|     | 9.5   | Learnings?                                           | 63 |
| **10** | **Conclusion** |                                              | **65** |
|     | 10.1  | Introduction                                         | 65 |
|     | 10.2  | Key Takeaways                                        | 66 |
|     | 10.3  | Future Challenges and Opportunities                  | 67 |
|     | 10.4  | Continuing Education and Resources                   | 67 |
|     | 10.5  | Discussion                                           | 68 |
|     | 10.6  | Closing Thoughts                                     | 69 |

# *Foreword*

In this foreword, I want to take a moment to frame the journey you're about to embark on—a journey through the evolving landscape of security as reshaped by artificial intelligence and machine learning. This book, authored by a passionate advocate of ethical technology use, serves as a bridge between complex technical concepts and their practical, ethical application in the real world. It's been a pleasure to witness the manuscript grow from a collection of ideas into a full-fledged guide that not only informs but also inspires action. The chapters ahead will not only deepen your understanding of AI and ML in security but also challenge you to think critically about how these powerful tools are shaped by—and can shape—the ethical frameworks within which we operate. This book is an essential read for anyone committed to the responsible development and deployment of technology in our society. As you turn each page, keep an open mind and consider not just the "how" of AI, but the "why" and the "what if" that accompany any transformative technological endeavor.

Happy learning!

# Part I

# Introduction

# 1

# Understanding Artificial Intelligence and Machine Learning

**CONTENTS**

| | | |
|---|---|---|
| 1.1 | What is Machine Learning? | 3 |
| 1.2 | How AI and ML Differ from Traditional Computing | 4 |
| 1.3 | Real-World Applications of AI and ML in Security | 4 |
| 1.4 | Engaging with the Concepts | 7 |
| | 1.4.1 Ethical Use of AI in Surveillance | 7 |
| | 1.4.2 Bias in Machine Learning Models | 7 |
| | 1.4.3 AI in Threat Detection and Response | 8 |
| | Future of AI and Quantum Computing in Security | 8 |
| | 1.4.4 Sustainable AI Deployment | 8 |
| 1.5 | Learnings? | 8 |
| | Key Learnings | 9 |

## 1.1 What is Machine Learning?

Welcome to the first chapter of your journey through the fascinating intersection of artificial intelligence (AI), machine learning (ML), and cybersecurity. This chapter is designed as your gateway into the world where algorithms not only mimic human cognition but also extend what humans alone can accomplish, especially in the area of security.

Artificial intelligence, at its core, is the science of making machines smart. It encompasses a broad range of technologies that enable machines to perceive, understand, act, and learn—activities that were traditionally thought to be exclusive to humans. Machine learning, a subset of AI, focuses on the ability of machines to receive a stream of data and learn from it, thereby improving their performance over time without being explicitly programmed.

Let's consider a simple example to illustrate this: spam filters in email systems. Initially, these systems were programmed with specific rules (like flagging emails containing certain words) to identify spam. However, with machine learning, email systems now continually learn from a variety of signals, such as which emails users mark as spam, and evolve their understanding of what constitutes spam based on new patterns emerging in the data.

## 1.2 How AI and ML Differ from Traditional Computing

Traditional computer programs operate in a pretty straightforward manner: they follow a set of strict, predefined rules and can only do what they've been specifically programmed to do. If we need them to do something new or different, a human has to step in and update the code manually. There's no flexibility, no learning—just the same rigid instructions being followed time and time again. But AI and ML systems, on the other hand, break away from this rigidity. They're designed to adapt and learn from the data they receive, finding patterns, making connections, and making decisions that aren't explicitly programmed into them. This learning capability is what makes them so powerful and transformative; they can evolve on their own, often with minimal human intervention.

To put it into perspective, think about the development of AI in autonomous vehicles. These vehicles are equipped with an array of sensors and cameras, constantly processing data to navigate the complexities of the road. They're not just passively taking in information—they're actively learning from it. Every mile driven, every stop sign recognized, every pedestrian avoided contributes to a vast pool of data that these AI systems use to refine their algorithms. This ongoing learning process allows the vehicles to improve their ability to make split-second decisions in real-world driving situations, like when to brake, how to swerve to avoid an obstacle, or even how to merge into busy traffic. Unlike traditional programs that would require a manual update for every new scenario, these AI systems adapt on the fly, becoming more accurate and reliable with each journey. However, this adaptability also introduces a level of unpredictability—how these systems might evolve isn't always something we can fully anticipate, which makes them both fascinating and, at times, a bit unnerving.

## 1.3 Real-World Applications of AI and ML in Security

In the world of security, artificial intelligence (AI) and machine learning (ML) are fundamentally changing the way we approach threat detection and response. To understand this shift, it's essential to first look at how security systems have traditionally worked. For a long time, the backbone of security relied heavily on static, rule-based systems. These systems operated by recognizing specific, predefined patterns of malicious activity, such as known virus signatures or identifiable behaviors that had been flagged as suspicious in the past. Essentially, they worked by comparing what was happening on a network or within a system to a catalog of known threats. If a match was found, the system would respond according to its programming, often by blocking the threat or alerting human operators to take action.

While this approach served its purpose well enough when threats were relatively straightforward and predictable, it has significant limitations in today's digital landscape. Modern threats are increasingly sophisticated, dynamic, and capable of morphing in ways that allow them to slip past these traditional defenses. Hackers are no longer just using basic viruses or predictable methods to breach systems; they're deploying complex, multi-layered attacks that can change their behavior in real-time to avoid detection. These advanced tactics can easily evade conventional security measures that are rooted in the "if this, then that" logic of traditional programming. For instance, a piece of malware might alter its code slightly each time it executes, rendering static detection methods largely ineffective.

This is where AI and ML step in to revolutionize the field of security. Unlike traditional systems, AI and ML do not require a predefined set of rules to operate. Instead, they learn and adapt from the vast amounts of data they process, continuously evolving their understanding of what constitutes a threat. Think of it like teaching a child to recognize danger—not by listing every single dangerous thing they might encounter but by helping them learn the general signs and cues of risk. In the same way, AI systems are trained on massive datasets that include network traffic, user behaviors, past security incidents, and even things like the normal day-to-day operations of a business. From this data, they learn to identify patterns and anomalies that might signal a security threat.

For example, an AI-driven security system can monitor millions of data points across a network, spotting unusual activities that might go unnoticed by human analysts or traditional security tools. This could include something like detecting a user downloading an unusually large volume of files at odd hours—behavior that doesn't fit with their normal usage patterns. In the past, this kind of subtle anomaly might have slipped through the cracks because it didn't match any known threat signature. But with AI, the system can immediately flag this activity as suspicious, triggering a response that could stop a potential data breach before it escalates. The AI isn't just looking for a specific threat; it's constantly learning what "normal" looks like and adapting to spot deviations from that baseline.

This adaptability is crucial because it allows AI and ML to keep up with the constantly changing tactics of attackers. Traditional security measures are like having a locked door with a specific key—effective until someone figures out a way to pick the lock or make a copy of the key. AI, on the other hand, is like having a guard that's always on duty, constantly learning new ways to spot intruders, and doesn't just rely on the same old lock and key. This guard is vigilant and always updating its methods based on the latest threats it has seen or learned about from others.

Moreover, AI-driven security systems are not just reactive—they can also be predictive. This means they don't just wait for something bad to happen before taking action. Instead, they can analyze historical data to identify patterns that might indicate an emerging threat, allowing security teams to act proactively. For instance, if an AI system detects a gradual increase in phishing attempts targeting a company's employees over time, it might predict that a larger, coordinated attack could be on the horizon. This insight can prompt the company to bolster its defenses in anticipation, rather than scrambling to respond after the fact.

However, as with any powerful tool, there are nuances and challenges that come with integrating AI and ML into security. One significant challenge is the sheer volume of data that these systems must process to be effective. Security AI needs to be trained on massive datasets to accurately distinguish between benign anomalies and true threats. This requires not only extensive computational resources but also careful calibration to avoid false positives—situations where normal activity is incorrectly flagged as suspicious. For instance, an AI system might detect that a CEO regularly logs into the company network late at night due to international travel, flagging this as a potential threat. If the system isn't fine-tuned, this could lead to unnecessary alarms and even disrupt legitimate business operations.

There's also the issue of transparency and understanding. AI systems, particularly those that rely on deep learning algorithms, can often operate as "black boxes," meaning that the reasoning behind their decisions isn't always clear to human users. This can be problematic in security, where understanding why a system has flagged a particular behavior as risky is crucial for taking the right actions. If an AI system raises an alert without a clear explanation, security teams might struggle to determine the best course of action—or worse, they might choose to ignore the alert altogether.

Another important consideration is the ethical dimension of using AI in security. While these technologies can dramatically improve our ability to detect and respond to threats, they also raise questions about privacy and the potential for misuse. AI systems that monitor network traffic and user behavior have access to vast amounts of sensitive data, and how this data is handled, stored, and protected is a critical concern. There's a fine line between using AI to safeguard digital environments and crossing into surveillance territory that could infringe on individual privacy rights. This balance is delicate, requiring robust policies and frameworks to ensure that AI-driven security measures are implemented responsibly.

Despite these challenges, the potential benefits of AI and ML in security are profound. These technologies offer a level of responsiveness, adaptability, and predictive power that traditional systems simply can't match. As cyber threats continue to evolve in complexity and scale, the ability to leverage AI to stay one step ahead is becoming increasingly crucial. In many ways, AI and ML are like a security team's secret weapon—a constantly evolving force that learns from every encounter, improves with every incident, and adapts to every new challenge.

In summary, AI and ML are transforming security by moving beyond the static, rule-based methods of the past. They offer a dynamic, adaptive approach that not only reacts to threats as they arise but also anticipates and learns from them, making security systems smarter and more effective over time. As we continue to refine these technologies and address the associated challenges, the potential to create safer digital environments becomes not just a possibility, but a reality that's already taking shape. The journey is ongoing, but with AI and ML at the helm, the future of security looks more robust and resilient than ever before.

## 1.4 Engaging with the Concepts

In this subsection, we invite you to engage more deeply with the concepts of artificial intelligence and machine learning by reflecting on their applications and implications in security. This exercise is designed to not only enhance your understanding but also to stimulate your critical thinking about the potential and challenges of AI technologies in security settings. Below are several topics for reflection. After contemplating each topic, we encourage you to jot down your thoughts, questions, or insights. Based on your inputs, we will explore potential solutions and discuss how these technologies can be optimally deployed in real-world scenarios.

### 1.4.1 Ethical Use of AI in Surveillance

**Reflection:** Consider the use of AI technologies in monitoring and surveillance. What are the potential benefits and risks associated with AI-driven surveillance systems in terms of privacy and security?
**Discussion:** How can we ensure that these systems are used responsibly? What guidelines or safeguards could be implemented to prevent abuse while maintaining public safety?

### 1.4.2 Bias in Machine Learning Models

**Reflection:** Reflect on the issue of bias in machine learning algorithms, especially those used in predictive policing or fraud detection. How can biased data affect the outcomes of AI systems? What are the consequences of these biases on individuals or communities?

**Discussion:** Explore solutions to mitigate bias in AI models. Consider techniques like diverse data collection, algorithm auditing, or transparency in AI deployments. How can these approaches help in creating fairer AI systems?

### 1.4.3 AI in Threat Detection and Response

**Reflection:** Think about the role of AI in identifying and responding to threats. What makes AI particularly suitable for this task? Are there limitations to what AI can achieve in the realm of threat detection?
**Discussion:** Discuss the integration of AI with traditional security measures. What synergies can be leveraged between human expertise and AI capabilities to enhance threat detection and response strategies?

### Future of AI and Quantum Computing in Security

**Reflection:** Quantum computing promises to bring significant changes to the field of security. Reflect on how quantum computing could impact AI-driven security solutions. What new opportunities and challenges might arise?
**Discussion:** Consider strategies to prepare for a future where quantum computing is mainstream. How should security professionals and organizations adapt to maintain robust defenses against quantum-enabled threats?

### 1.4.4 Sustainable AI Deployment

**Reflection:** As AI systems become more prevalent, their environmental impact becomes more significant. Reflect on the sustainability of deploying large-scale AI systems in terms of energy consumption and electronic waste.
**Discussion:** What measures can be taken to make AI deployments more sustainable? Discuss the role of energy-efficient algorithms, hardware optimizations, or policies that promote greener AI technologies.

This interactive reflection section is designed to be a dialogic platform between you, the reader, and the evolving landscape of AI and ML in security. Your insights and inputs are invaluable as we navigate these complex topics together, seeking solutions that are not only technologically sound but also ethically robust and socially responsible.

## 1.5 Learnings?

As we near the conclusion of this chapter, it's important to pause and reflect on the key learnings we've gathered. This book goes beyond being just a collection of facts and theories about artificial intelligence and machine learning in security; it's a carefully crafted guide filled with practical insights and forward-thinking ideas. Throughout our journey, we've established a solid foundation by defining AI and ML, helping us understand their potential impact on security practices. We've explored AI's significant role in processing and analyzing data far beyond human capabilities, making it a vital tool for detecting and responding to threats with unprecedented efficiency. However, our exploration also highlighted the crucial ethical considerations of AI deployment, particularly the privacy risks and moral dilemmas that come with it. We examined the challenges posed by biases in machine learning models, emphasizing the importance of diverse training data and transparency in algorithms to avoid unfair outcomes.

We've also discussed the integration of AI into traditional security frameworks, showing how these advanced technologies can complement and enhance existing methods, thereby preparing organizations for more complex threats. Looking to the future, we touched upon the potential impacts of emerging technologies like quantum computing on security, stressing the need for preparedness in this evolving field. Finally, the theme of sustainability in AI deployment was a recurring topic, reminding us of the environmental and societal impacts of these technologies and the importance of a responsible approach to their implementation. This chapter, and indeed the entire book, is designed to empower you with the knowledge to make informed decisions and innovate responsibly in the dynamic world of AI and ML in security. As we move forward, let these learnings serve as your guide through the complex yet exciting landscape of AI-driven security.

**Key Learnings**

- Understanding the Fundamentals
- Appreciation of AI's Role in Security
- Ethical Considerations are Crucial
- The Challenge of Bias
- Integrative Strategies for Security
- Future-Ready Approaches
- Sustainable and Responsible AI Deployment

# 2

## Foundational Technologies

**CONTENTS**

| | | |
|---|---|---|
| 2.1 | What Will We Learn? | 11 |
| 2.2 | What Are These ML Algorithms | 12 |
| 2.3 | Neural Networks and Deep Learning in Security | 13 |
| 2.4 | Data Processing and Analysing Techniques | 14 |
| 2.5 | Discussion | 15 |
| 2.6 | Learnings? | 16 |

## 2.1 What Will We Learn?

In this second chapter, we embark on a deeper journey into the core technologies that drive artificial intelligence and machine learning in security. This is where we get to the nuts and bolts of how these advanced systems work—delving into the specific algorithms, data processing techniques, and neural networks that serve as the backbone of intelligent security solutions. We'll break down the key components that allow AI and ML to function effectively, from the basics of how algorithms process vast amounts of data to identify patterns, to the sophisticated neural networks that mimic the way the human brain learns and adapts. Understanding these foundational elements is crucial because they are what make AI-driven security systems not just possible, but incredibly powerful. For example, when we talk about algorithms, we're referring to the sets of rules and calculations that enable these systems to sift through oceans of data, pinpointing anomalies that could signal a threat. Similarly, data processing techniques allow these systems to handle the sheer volume and variety of information that flows through modern digital environments. And at the heart of it all are neural networks, which can learn and evolve over time, improving their accuracy and efficiency in detecting and responding to threats. By exploring these technologies, we gain a clearer picture of the complexity and potential of AI in security. This knowledge equips us not just to understand the systems at a surface level, but to appreciate the ingenuity and sophistication that go into creating them. It also prepares us to critically assess how these technologies are deployed, ensuring that we can leverage their strengths while being mindful of their limitations. So, as we move through this chapter, we're not just learning about the mechanics of AI and ML; we're building the foundation for a deeper engagement with the future of security—one where technology and innovation play a pivotal role in safeguarding our digital world.

## 2.2 What Are These ML Algorithms

Understanding machine learning algorithms might sound a bit technical at first, but let's break it down into something much easier to digest—almost like explaining it to a friend who's just starting to learn about these things. Machine learning algorithms are like the brains behind AI systems. Imagine them as little engines that power these systems, allowing them to learn from data, just like how we learn from experiences. These algorithms help the AI make smart decisions, almost like teaching a robot how to recognize a cat by showing it hundreds of pictures of cats and dogs and helping it figure out the difference. Let's explore some of the main types of machine learning algorithms used in security, step by step.

First, there's something called Supervised Learning. Think of it like having a teacher who knows all the answers. In this kind of learning, the AI gets to learn from a dataset where the correct answers are already known. It's a bit like doing homework with an answer key in the back of the book—you can always check if you're getting it right. For example, in security, this might look like showing the AI a bunch of files and telling it, "Hey, these ones are safe, but those ones over there are dangerous malware." Over time, the AI learns to spot the dangerous ones on its own, just by comparing new files to what it has seen before. It's like teaching a kid to recognize which mushrooms are safe to eat by showing them pictures of safe and poisonous ones.

Next up is Unsupervised Learning, which is a bit more adventurous because there's no teacher around to give the right answers. Instead, the AI has to figure things out all by itself, kind of like exploring a new game without any instructions. In unsupervised learning, the AI looks for patterns and tries to group things based on what it observes. It's like when you're at a party and you notice that all the kids who like sports are hanging out together, and the kids who like reading are in another corner—you're figuring out these groups without anyone telling you. In security, unsupervised learning might be used for anomaly detection, which is just a fancy way of saying it's looking for anything unusual. For example, if an AI notices that someone is suddenly downloading a ton of files in the middle of the night when they usually don't, it might flag that as suspicious, because it doesn't fit the normal pattern.

*Foundational Technologies* 13

Finally, there's Reinforcement Learning, which is kind of like training a puppy. Imagine you're teaching a dog to fetch a ball. Every time the puppy brings the ball back, you give it a treat. If it runs off with the ball instead, you don't reward it, and maybe you even gently correct it. Over time, the puppy learns that bringing the ball back gets it treats, so it keeps doing that. Reinforcement learning works similarly. It's all about giving the AI a set of rewards and penalties to help it learn the best actions to take. In the world of security, this could mean training an AI to optimize security protocols—basically figuring out the best way to keep things safe by trying different strategies and learning which ones work best. It's like playing a game where you get points for doing the right things and lose points for mistakes, and the AI is always trying to beat its high score by getting better and better at protecting against threats.So, these algorithms—supervised, unsupervised, and reinforcement learning—are like different learning styles that help AI systems become smarter over time. They allow AI to take in vast amounts of data, learn from it, and make decisions that help keep us safe in the digital world. By understanding these types of learning, we start to see how AI can be such a powerful tool, not just a mysterious technology, but something that learns and grows, just like us.

## 2.3 Neural Networks and Deep Learning in Security

Neural networks, especially deep learning models, are like the superheroes of AI when it comes to security. They're designed to mimic the way our brains work, making them incredibly good at processing and understanding huge amounts of data. Imagine them as super-smart robots that can quickly make sense of complex information, picking out important details just like our brains do when we try to solve puzzles or recognize faces in a crowd. Let's dive into a couple of key types of neural networks that play a big role in security, and I'll explain it in a way that's as simple as possible.

First up are Convolutional Neural Networks (CNNs). Think of CNNs as the specialists for visual data—they're like AI with super eyesight. These networks are amazing at analyzing images and videos because they can look at the details, like colors, shapes, and textures, and figure out what's important. It's similar to how we look at a picture and instantly recognize whether it's a cat or a dog, even if we've never seen that exact picture before. In security, CNNs are used to automatically analyze surveillance footage. So instead of a person staring at camera feeds all day, a CNN can watch the footage and alert us if it sees something unusual, like a person walking into a restricted area or an object left unattended. This makes security systems much more efficient and reliable, because the AI can watch multiple cameras at once without getting tired or distracted.

Then we have Recurrent Neural Networks (RNNs), which are the go-to experts for anything that happens over time. They're designed to remember things from one moment to the next, making them perfect for looking at sequences—like a story being told one chapter at a time. Imagine reading a mystery novel; you need to remember clues from earlier chapters to figure out the ending. RNNs do the same thing, but with data. In security, RNNs are used to spot patterns in things that happen over time, like network traffic or user behavior. For example, if someone's logging into their account from New York, then suddenly from London an hour later, an RNN can flag that as suspicious because it remembers the sequence of logins and knows that's not normal behavior.

These networks are particularly powerful because they don't just look at one piece of data in isolation—they connect the dots, much like how we connect events in our daily lives. For instance, if you normally use your computer in the morning and then suddenly start using it at odd hours, an RNN can catch that change in pattern and raise a red flag. It's like having a super-alert assistant who not only watches what you do but also remembers how you usually do things and warns you if something seems off.Neural networks, whether it's CNNs for images or RNNs for sequences, are like having specialized tools in a high-tech security toolbox. They allow AI systems to go beyond basic checks and instead understand the context of what's happening, making them incredibly valuable for keeping digital spaces safe. By leveraging the strengths of these networks, security systems can become smarter and more responsive, handling tasks that would be impossible for humans to manage alone. This means not just spotting threats faster but also being able to adapt and learn over time, making these AI-driven systems an essential part of modern security.

## 2.4 Data Processing and Analysing Techniques

Data processing and analysis are like the behind-the-scenes work that makes AI systems actually useful in real-world situations, especially in security. Think of it as setting up the stage before the main performance. If you don't get the setup right, the whole show can fall apart, no matter how talented the performers are. For AI, this setup involves a few key stages that are all about getting the data ready so the AI can do its job properly. Let's walk through these stages in a way that makes sense even if you're not a tech expert.

First, there's Data Collection. Imagine you're collecting puzzle pieces from all over the place to build a big picture. In AI for security, data collection means gathering raw information from various sources, like network traffic logs that track what's happening on a network, user activity records that show how people are using systems, or threat databases that keep a list of

*Foundational Technologies* 15

known dangers. It's a bit like a detective gathering clues from multiple crime scenes to solve a case. The more pieces you collect, the clearer the picture becomes, but you also need to make sure you're gathering the right kinds of pieces. Too little or too much irrelevant data can be like having random puzzle pieces that don't fit together.Next is Data Cleaning, which is basically tidying up all the data you've collected. Think of it like going through a bunch of old photographs and picking out the ones that are clear and relevant, while tossing out the blurry or unrelated ones. In the world of AI, data cleaning involves preprocessing the data to remove errors, duplicates, or irrelevant information. This step is super important because messy data can lead to inaccurate results, just like how a smudged photograph can give you the wrong impression. For example, if the data includes incorrect timestamps or corrupted entries, it might confuse the AI, causing it to make mistakes. So, data cleaning is all about making sure everything is in good shape before the AI starts learning from it.

After cleaning, we move on to Feature Extraction. This step is a bit like highlighting the most important parts of a book to study for a test—you're picking out the key details that are most likely to help you understand the whole story. In AI, feature extraction means transforming the raw, cleaned data into a format that's suitable for machine learning models to use. It's about selecting the specific attributes that are most indicative of what you're looking for—in this case, potential security threats. For example, instead of just throwing all the network data at the AI, you might extract features like the frequency of failed login attempts, unusual access times, or large data transfers. These features are like the key clues that can help the AI identify suspicious activity. Feature extraction is critical because it boils down the vast sea of data into the most relevant parts, making it easier and faster for the AI to process. It's a bit like giving a detective a summary of the most crucial evidence rather than making them sift through every single detail from every case ever recorded. By focusing on the most telling features, AI can make smarter, quicker decisions about what constitutes a threat.Overall, these stages of data processing—collection, cleaning, and feature extraction—are what make AI systems reliable and effective in security. They ensure that the AI isn't just working with a chaotic jumble of information but is instead being fed clean, relevant data that highlights the most important patterns and clues. It's all about setting the AI up for success, giving it the best chance to do its job well and keep our digital environments safe.

## 2.5 Discussion

Interactive discussions can be a great way to bring these concepts to life, especially when thinking about how AI technologies can be practically applied in your own security efforts. Let's take a step back and imagine how you might use these tools in real-world scenarios, whether for a project you're working on or just exploring the possibilities. Here are some questions to guide your reflection. Take your time with each one, and feel free to write down your thoughts or even discuss them with colleagues or peers.

First, consider which type of machine learning algorithm might be the most effective for a new cybersecurity application you have in mind. Are you dealing with clear, labeled data where supervised learning could shine? Or perhaps you're tackling something more exploratory, where unsupervised learning would be better at finding hidden patterns? Maybe you're in a situation where continuous adaptation is key, making reinforcement learning the best fit. Think about the specific needs of your application and how different algorithms could meet those needs.Next, reflect on how neural networks could enhance your current security systems. For instance, could convolutional neural networks help with analyzing visual data like security footage, making the process faster and more accurate? Or might recurrent neural networks be useful in monitoring ongoing patterns in network traffic to catch subtle, evolving threats? At the same time, it's important to think about potential pitfalls—like the high computational power neural networks often require, or the challenge of interpreting their complex decision-making processes. How would you balance the benefits with these challenges?Finally, think about the data collection and processing stages, which are often the backbone of any AI application in security. What challenges do you anticipate in gathering and preparing your data? Perhaps it's the sheer volume of data, or the difficulty in accessing reliable sources. Maybe it's the time-consuming process of cleaning and organizing data to make it usable. Consider practical ways to tackle these issues, whether it's through automated data cleaning tools, collaborating with other teams for better data access, or even scaling your resources to handle large datasets more effectively.

By reflecting on these questions, you'll start to see how AI can be tailored to fit your specific needs in security, as well as the hurdles you might need to overcome to implement these technologies successfully. Engaging with these ideas not only helps solidify your understanding but also empowers you to think creatively and strategically about the future of AI in your own security practices.

## 2.6 Learnings?

Key learnings and reflections from this chapter have given us a closer look at the inner workings of AI and ML technologies that play a critical role in security. Let's take a moment to summarize what we've covered and why it matters.

- Choosing the right machine learning algorithm based on specific security needs.

- Leveraging deep learning models for analyzing complex data sets in security.

- Ensuring quality data processing and preparation for effective AI performance.

- Integrating AI to build robust and adaptive security systems.

- Using insights to drive innovation and improvement in AI-driven security.

# 3

# Fundamentals of Machine Learning

**CONTENTS**

| 3.1 | Implementation Strategies | 19 |
| --- | --- | --- |
| 3.2 | Integrating AI into Existing Security Frameworks | 20 |
| 3.3 | Building AI-Driven Security Tools | 21 |
| 3.4 | Automating Threat Detection and Response | 22 |
| 3.5 | Discussion | 23 |
| 3.6 | Thinking | 24 |

## 3.1 Implementation Strategies

In this chapter, we shift gears from the theoretical foundations we've explored earlier to focus on practical, hands-on strategies for bringing AI and ML technologies into your security frameworks. This section is all about making the leap from understanding the concepts to actually applying them in real-world scenarios. We'll walk you through how to integrate these advanced, intelligent systems into your current security setups, ensuring that they don't just add complexity but truly enhance and strengthen your defenses. Think of this chapter as your guide to merging the power of AI with your existing security measures. We'll explore step-by-step approaches to implementation, covering everything from selecting the right AI tools for your specific needs to addressing the common challenges that can arise during integration. Whether you're looking to boost threat detection capabilities, automate responses, or simply make your security systems more adaptive and intelligent, this chapter provides the practical insights you need to make it happen.

By focusing on how to effectively embed AI and ML into your security operations, we aim to help you create a more resilient and forward-looking defense strategy. This isn't just about adding new technology for the sake of it; it's about thoughtfully incorporating AI in ways that complement and enhance what you already have in place. As we go through this segment, you'll gain a clearer understanding of how to leverage these tools to not only keep pace with evolving threats but also to stay ahead of them, ensuring your cybersecurity measures are as robust and effective as possible.

## 3.2 Integrating AI into Existing Security Frameworks

Integrating AI into your existing security frameworks isn't as simple as just installing a new piece of software or running a fancy new algorithm—it's about building a harmonious relationship where AI works hand-in-hand with your current protocols. Think of it as adding a new team member who brings advanced skills to your group but needs to mesh well with how things are already done. Here's a step-by-step guide on how you can start weaving AI into your security operations effectively.First, you'll want to begin with an Assessment of Current Systems. This step is like taking a close look at your existing security measures, almost like an inventory check. The goal here is to identify where your current defenses might have gaps or areas that could use a boost. For example, maybe your system struggles with detecting certain types of threats quickly enough, or perhaps there's too much manual work involved in monitoring network activity. Understanding these weak spots helps you see where AI could have the biggest impact, making your overall security stronger and more efficient.Next, it's time to move on to Choosing the Right AI Solutions. Based on your assessment, you'll need to decide which AI tools are the best fit for your specific needs. This might involve comparing different types of machine learning algorithms—like deciding whether supervised learning for specific threat detection or unsupervised learning for anomaly detection would serve you better. You'll also have to consider whether it's best to go with a pre-built AI solution that's ready to go out of the box or if a custom-built model tailored to your unique requirements would provide more value. It's about finding the right tool for the right job, ensuring that the AI you integrate is truly enhancing your security framework.

Once you've selected your AI solutions, the next step is Pilot Testing. Rather than jumping straight into a full-scale implementation, it's wise to start small. Think of this like a trial run where you can test how well the AI integrates with your existing systems. During this pilot phase, closely monitor the AI's performance—how effectively it's identifying threats, how smoothly it's working with your current protocols, and what kind of feedback you're getting from the people who use it daily. This testing phase is crucial because it gives you the opportunity to spot any hiccups early on and make necessary adjustments before rolling out the AI across your entire operation. It's much easier to tweak and improve on a small scale than to fix problems after a full launch.By following these steps—assessing your current systems, choosing the right AI tools, and conducting pilot tests—you can create a more seamless and effective integration of AI into your security frameworks. The goal is to ensure that AI doesn't just become an add-on but a true enhancement that works in tandem with your existing measures, making your overall security operations smarter, faster, and more adaptive to the ever-evolving landscape of threats.

## 3.3 Building AI-Driven Security Tools

Building your own AI-driven security tools can be an incredibly rewarding process because it allows you to create customized solutions that are tailored specifically to your unique security challenges. It's like crafting a suit of armor that fits perfectly—not too tight, not too loose, but just right for the kinds of threats you face. This approach gives you the flexibility to address specific vulnerabilities and adapt the tools as your needs evolve. Here's a step-by-step guide on how to get started with creating your own AI-driven security tools.

The first step is Tool Development. Before you dive into the technical work, you need to clearly define what you want your tool to do. Think about the specific threats or vulnerabilities that are most concerning for your organization. Is it about detecting phishing attempts, spotting unusual behavior in network traffic, or perhaps securing sensitive data against unauthorized access? Clearly defining the scope and objectives of your tool helps set the direction for the entire project. Once you know what you're aiming to achieve, it's time to assemble a team with the right mix of skills—people who understand machine learning, cybersecurity, data science, and software development. Having a strong, diverse team is like having the right ingredients for a recipe; each person's expertise contributes to building a tool that's effective and reliable.

Next comes the Data Training phase. This is where you gather and prepare the data that your AI tool will learn from. Think of this step as laying the foundation for a building—if the foundation isn't solid, the whole structure is at risk. The data you collect should be relevant to the threats you're targeting and should be as clean and accurate as possible. This might involve pulling in data from security logs, past incident reports, or other relevant sources. But just gathering data isn't enough; it needs to be preprocessed, which means cleaning it up, removing errors, and making sure it's formatted in a way that the AI can understand. The quality of this data is crucial because it directly impacts how well your tool will perform. Poor quality data can lead to inaccurate models that miss threats or raise too many false alarms, so it's worth investing the time and effort to get this part right.

Finally, you'll move on to Model Training and Evaluation. This is where the actual AI magic happens. You'll develop and train your model using the prepared data, teaching it to recognize patterns and make decisions based on what it has learned. But training the model is just the beginning—you'll also need to continuously evaluate its performance. This means running tests to see how accurately it detects threats, tweaking the algorithms as needed, and fine-tuning the model until it consistently meets your standards. It's a bit like training an athlete; it takes time, practice, and adjustments to reach peak performance. You might have to go back and refine your data or adjust the model's parameters, but this iterative process is key to developing a tool that not only works well in theory but also holds up in real-world situations.

## 3.4 Automating Threat Detection and Response

Automating threat detection and response is like giving your security operations a powerful boost, allowing you to catch and respond to threats much faster and more accurately than you could manually. It's all about making your security smarter and more proactive, so instead of waiting for someone to notice a problem, your system can automatically detect and deal with issues as they arise. Here's a guide on how to get started with implementing automation in your threat detection and response processes.

The first step is Setting Parameters. This is where you define exactly what counts as a threat and decide how your system should react when it detects one. It's like setting the rules for a game—you need clear guidelines on what triggers an alert and what actions should be taken in response. For example, you might set thresholds for certain types of behavior, like an unusually high number of login attempts or data being accessed from unfamiliar locations. Depending on the severity of the threat, your automated system can be programmed to take specific actions, such as sending an alert to the security team, blocking suspicious IP addresses, or even shutting down access to certain parts of the network. By clearly defining these parameters, you ensure that your system knows exactly what to look for and how to respond without needing human intervention every time.

Next, you'll need to focus on Integration with Existing Systems. Automation works best when it's fully integrated with your current security infrastructure. This means making sure your automated threat detection and response tools are connected to other key components like firewalls, intrusion detection systems, and monitoring tools. Think of it like assembling a team where everyone needs to work together seamlessly—each part of your security setup should communicate effectively with the others to coordinate a unified response to threats. For instance, if an automated system detects a potential breach, it needs to work with your firewall to block the intruder and with your alerting system to notify the right people. Integration helps ensure that all parts of your security are aligned and working together, making your overall response more effective and efficient.

The final piece of the puzzle is Continuous Learning. Threats are always evolving, and what worked yesterday might not be effective tomorrow. That's

*Fundamentals of Machine Learning* 23

why it's important to set up your automated systems to continuously learn and adapt. This involves feeding the system new data about emerging threats and teaching it from past experiences, including any false alarms. For example, if the system incorrectly flags a legitimate action as a threat, it should learn from that mistake and refine its parameters to avoid similar false positives in the future. Similarly, as new types of attacks emerge, your system should update its understanding and adjust its responses accordingly. It's a bit like training a guard dog that learns over time not just to bark at everything, but to recognize specific, real dangers and respond appropriately.

## 3.5 Discussion

Let's take a moment to think about how AI could enhance your organization's approach to security. Engaging in an interactive discussion around these ideas can help you identify practical ways to integrate AI into your existing security measures. Here are some reflection points to consider, each aimed at sparking ideas about how AI might fit into your organization's unique security landscape.

First, consider the existing security challenges your organization faces that could be addressed with AI. Are there specific pain points, like difficulty in detecting sophisticated threats, dealing with a high volume of alerts, or managing data breaches effectively? Reflect on how AI could step in to help, perhaps by automating routine tasks, identifying patterns that might be missed by traditional methods, or providing deeper insights into potential vulnerabilities. Think about the steps you would need to take to implement AI solutions—such as evaluating your current systems, selecting the right AI tools, or piloting a small-scale integration to start.Next, imagine if you were to build a custom AI tool tailored specifically to your organization's security needs. What features would you want this tool to have? For example, would it focus on predictive threat analysis, real-time monitoring, or advanced anomaly detection? Think about why these features would be important for your specific context and how they could help address the unique challenges you face. Maybe you'd want a tool that not only detects threats but also provides actionable recommendations for mitigating them, or one that integrates seamlessly with your existing security infrastructure to enhance overall efficiency.

Lastly, consider how automation could transform your organization's response to security threats. Automation has the potential to change the game by speeding up response times, reducing human error, and allowing your security team to focus on more strategic tasks. Reflect on how automated systems could be set up to handle different types of incidents—whether it's automatically blocking suspicious activity, alerting the right people at the right time, or even taking preventive measures before a threat fully materializes. However, implementing automation also comes with its own set of challenges, so think about what measures you would take to ensure that your automation is both effective and reliable. This might involve regular testing, setting clear thresholds for actions, or having manual overrides in place for critical situations.By reflecting on these points, you can start to see where AI might fit within your organization's security strategy and how it could help tackle some of the biggest challenges you're facing. This discussion isn't just about imagining possibilities—it's about finding practical ways to make your security smarter, more efficient, and better equipped to handle the complexities of today's digital threats.

## 3.6 Thinking

This chapter has been pivotal in transitioning from understanding AI and ML technologies to applying them effectively in cybersecurity practices. Here are the key takeaways:

- Importance of aligning AI with existing cybersecurity frameworks.

- Steps for developing tailored AI-driven security tools.

- Enhancing speed and accuracy in threat detection and response.

- Adapting systems to learn from new threats and false positives.

- Integrating AI without disrupting current operations.

# 4

# Real Life Case Studies

**CONTENTS**

| | | |
|---|---|---|
| 4.1 | Introduction ................................................... | 25 |
| 4.2 | Retail Sector: Preventing Fraud with Machine Learning? ....... | 26 |
| 4.3 | Healthcare: Protecting Sensitive Data through AI .............. | 27 |
| 4.4 | Government: National Security Enhancements with AI ......... | 28 |
| 4.5 | AI Failures in Security ........................................ | 29 |
| 4.6 | Discussion ..................................................... | 31 |
| 4.7 | Learnings ...................................................... | 32 |

## 4.1 Introduction

In this chapter, we dive into the real-world applications of AI and ML in security, exploring detailed case studies that show how these advanced technologies are being leveraged to bolster security measures across different industries. By looking at specific examples, we get a clear view of the practical implications, challenges, and successes that come with integrating AI into security strategies. These case studies aren't just about showcasing what's possible—they're about understanding the tangible impact that AI can have on enhancing security in everyday scenarios.

Each case study serves as a learning tool, providing valuable insights into how AI and ML are applied to solve real security problems. For instance, you might see how AI is used to detect fraud in financial transactions, protect sensitive data in healthcare, or safeguard critical infrastructure in industries like energy and manufacturing. By breaking down these examples, we can learn about the different approaches taken, the obstacles faced along the way, and the innovative solutions that helped overcome them. This hands-on perspective makes it easier to grasp the complexities of AI in security and highlights the potential benefits that can be achieved.

Beyond just learning from these examples, these case studies also serve as a source of inspiration. They show that the integration of AI into security isn't just a theoretical concept—it's happening now, and it's making a difference. Whether it's through automated threat detection, predictive analytics, or advanced anomaly detection, AI is proving to be a game-changer in the field of security. As you go through these case studies, think about how similar strategies could be applied within your own organization. What lessons can you take away? What ideas spark a sense of possibility for enhancing your own security measures? By examining these real-world applications, you're not just observing from the sidelines—you're equipping yourself with the knowledge and inspiration needed to drive innovation in your own security strategies.

## 4.2 Retail Sector: Preventing Fraud with Machine Learning?

In the retail sector, fraud is a persistent challenge that can take on many forms, including credit card fraud, return fraud, and even loyalty program abuse. To combat these issues, many retailers are turning to machine learning as a powerful tool for detecting and preventing fraudulent activities. Machine learning models can analyze vast amounts of data related to transactions and customer behavior, helping to spot unusual patterns that might indicate fraud.One example comes from a major retail company that decided to implement a machine learning model to enhance its fraud detection capabilities. Instead of relying on traditional, rule-based systems that often miss new fraud tactics or generate a high number of false alarms, the company adopted a more dynamic approach. They developed a machine learning model that scans transactions in real time, continuously analyzing patterns to identify any deviations from the norm. By using supervised learning, the model was trained on historical data of both legitimate and fraudulent transactions, allowing it to learn what typical behavior looks like and what might be considered suspicious.

As the system operates, it doesn't stay static; it continuously learns and adapts from new data. This means that as new types of fraud emerge, the model can quickly incorporate these into its understanding, staying one step ahead of fraudsters. The result? Within the first six months of implementing this AI-driven approach, the company saw a 30% reduction in fraudulent transactions. This significant decrease not only helped protect the company's bottom line but also boosted customer trust and satisfaction. Additionally, because the machine learning model is designed to adapt and refine its detection criteria, it was able to reduce the number of false positives—those frustrating instances where legitimate transactions are incorrectly flagged as fraud. This adaptability made the system far more efficient and effective than older, static rule-based methods.Overall, this case highlights how machine learning can be a game-changer in the fight against fraud in the retail sector. By leveraging real-time data analysis and adaptive learning, the company not only improved its ability to detect fraud but also made the entire process more efficient, reducing unnecessary disruptions for genuine customers. It's a great example of how AI and machine learning can be tailored to meet the specific challenges of an industry, delivering tangible results that go beyond just theory and into real-world impact.

## 4.3 Healthcare: Protecting Sensitive Data through AI

Healthcare institutions are often prime targets for cyberattacks because they handle highly sensitive information, such as patient medical records and personal health data. The consequences of a data breach in this sector can be severe, including financial loss, compromised patient privacy, and damage to the institution's reputation. To bolster their defenses, many healthcare providers are turning to AI and machine learning to enhance their security protocols and improve anomaly detection.One healthcare provider took a proactive step by implementing an AI-driven security system specifically designed to monitor access to sensitive data. This system employs unsupervised learning algorithms, which are particularly effective for this task because they don't rely on predefined rules or labeled data. Instead, the system learns what normal access patterns look like—such as when and how authorized personnel typically access certain types of data—and uses this understanding to spot anything that deviates from the norm. For instance, if the AI detects that a user is accessing an unusually large amount of patient data or is trying to access records at odd hours, it flags these actions as potential security threats.

The implementation of this AI-driven system had a significant impact. It was able to identify several unauthorized access attempts in real time, allowing the healthcare provider to respond immediately and prevent potential data breaches. This real-time detection and response capability is crucial in healthcare, where even a brief delay can lead to significant exposure of sensitive information. Moreover, the system's continuous learning feature means that it doesn't just rely on a static understanding of normal behavior. As it processes more data and encounters different scenarios, it refines its ability to distinguish between legitimate and suspicious activities. Over time, this dynamic learning reduces the number of false alarms, which can otherwise cause unnecessary disruptions and pull valuable resources away from other critical tasks.This case underscores the value of AI in protecting sensitive data within the healthcare sector. By leveraging unsupervised learning and real-time anomaly detection, the healthcare provider was able to not only enhance their security posture but also ensure that their data protection measures keep pace with evolving threats. The continuous improvement of the AI model's accuracy further ensures that security efforts remain efficient, minimizing the impact of false positives while effectively safeguarding patient data. This approach demonstrates how AI can be a powerful ally in the ongoing effort to protect sensitive information in environments where privacy and security are paramount.

## 4.4 Government: National Security Enhancements with AI

National security agencies are tasked with the enormous responsibility of monitoring and responding to a wide variety of threats, ranging from cyber espionage to terrorist communications. Given the sheer volume and complexity of data that these agencies must analyze, traditional methods often fall short in terms of speed and efficiency. This is where AI steps in as a game-changer, providing the tools necessary to process massive datasets rapidly and accurately, thereby enhancing national security efforts.

One national security agency took a major step forward by implementing an AI-driven system designed to sift through vast amounts of communication data. This system employs a combination of natural language processing (NLP) and pattern recognition algorithms, which work together to scan and analyze communications for signs of suspicious activity. NLP allows the AI to understand and interpret human language, identifying key phrases or patterns that could indicate potential threats, such as coded messages or unusual communication patterns. Meanwhile, pattern recognition algorithms help the system learn to detect behaviors or sequences of events that align with known security risks.

The implementation of this AI system has had a significant impact on the agency's ability to manage and respond to threats. It has proven instrumental in identifying numerous potential security threats that might have otherwise gone unnoticed amid the overwhelming sea of data. One of the key strengths of the AI system is its ability to differentiate between false leads and genuine security concerns, which is crucial for focusing resources on real threats rather than chasing down harmless anomalies. Moreover, the AI's capacity for continuous learning allows it to refine its detection capabilities over time. By learning from past incidents—both successful threat identifications and false alarms—the system becomes more adept at recognizing what constitutes a true threat, enhancing its overall accuracy and reliability.

This approach not only improves the agency's response times but also increases the precision of threat detection, allowing for quicker and more targeted interventions. The AI system's ability to evolve with new data and adapt to emerging threats makes it an invaluable tool in the constantly changing landscape of national security. Overall, this case highlights the transformative potential of AI in government operations, demonstrating how advanced tech-

*Real Life Case Studies* 29

nologies can significantly enhance the efficiency and effectiveness of national security measures, keeping nations safer in an increasingly complex world.

## 4.5 AI Failures in Security

Artificial intelligence (AI) has revolutionized the field of security, offering unprecedented capabilities in threat detection, response automation, and overall security management. However, AI is not without its shortcomings, and understanding its failures is crucial to building more resilient and reliable systems. This chapter delves into real-life scenarios where AI has failed in security contexts, analyzing the reasons behind these failures and highlighting key lessons that can be applied to future AI deployments. These case studies not only showcase the potential risks associated with AI but also offer invaluable insights into how these systems can be improved. One prominent example of AI failure in security is Tesla's Autopilot system and its issue of phantom braking. Tesla's Autopilot, an AI-driven advanced driver assistance system, has faced numerous incidents where it failed to correctly interpret road conditions. Phantom braking occurs when the system suddenly applies brakes without any apparent reason, mistaking harmless objects or shadows for obstacles. The reasons for this failure are multifaceted. Firstly, there is an overreliance on machine vision; the Autopilot system relies heavily on cameras and machine vision, which can misinterpret visual data due to poor weather, low lighting, or unusual objects on the road. Secondly, there is a lack of redundancy in the sensor system; the absence of additional sensors like LIDAR, which could provide another layer of environmental understanding, contributed to the system's vulnerability. Finally, insufficient testing under real-world conditions meant that the system did not cover all the edge cases that drivers encounter, such as unusual lighting conditions or unexpected road layouts. From this case study, several lessons can be drawn: enhancing sensor fusion by incorporating multiple types of sensors, such as radar and LIDAR, can significantly improve the AI's ability to accurately interpret its surroundings. Moreover, robust testing in diverse conditions is essential for AI systems in security to ensure reliability across a wide range of scenarios. Lastly, while automation can enhance safety, human oversight remains crucial, especially in complex and unpredictable environments, to mitigate the risks associated with AI-driven decision-making.

Another notable case study involves Microsoft's Tay chatbot, which illustrates the susceptibility of AI systems to social engineering. In 2016, Microsoft launched Tay, an AI chatbot designed to engage with people on Twitter. However, within 24 hours, Tay began spewing offensive and inappropriate content after being manipulated by users who exploited its machine learning algorithms. The failure of Tay can be attributed to several key factors. The chatbot was highly vulnerable to adversarial inputs; Tay's algorithms were not equipped to filter out or appropriately respond to harmful or misleading inputs, making it easy for malicious users to manipulate the system. Additionally, there was a lack of content moderation, as the system had insufficient oversight of the interactions, allowing the chatbot to learn and replicate toxic behaviors without any checks. Finally, the reliance on unsupervised learning without adequate safeguards meant that Tay was highly susceptible to manipulation by a small but active group of users who could significantly influence its outputs. To prevent such failures, AI systems should have built-in content filters and moderation tools to prevent the propagation of harmful or false information. Moreover, deploying supervised learning models, especially when AI is used in sensitive areas like security, can help ensure that the system learns appropriate behaviors. Continuous monitoring of AI behavior and the capability to intervene quickly can prevent small issues from escalating into significant failures, highlighting the importance of real-time oversight in AI deployments.

Facial recognition technology in law enforcement provides another critical example of AI failure in security, particularly concerning biases in AI models. Facial recognition systems deployed by several police departments have been criticized for their inaccuracies, especially in identifying people of color, which in some cases has led to wrongful arrests. The primary reasons for these failures include bias in training data; many facial recognition systems were trained on datasets that lacked sufficient diversity, resulting in lower accuracy rates for minority groups. Moreover, there was a lack of transparency and accountability in the deployment of these systems, with few mechanisms in place for auditing the accuracy and fairness of the AI models. This lack of oversight allowed these systems to be used despite known issues with their reliability and bias. Furthermore, law enforcement agencies often overestimated the capabilities of facial recognition technology, relying on it for critical decisions without fully understanding its limitations and the potential for significant errors. To address these issues, AI systems in security must be trained on diverse and representative datasets to reduce bias and improve accuracy. Regular audits and bias testing are essential to ensure that the AI system's decisions are fair and equitable, and limiting the use of facial recognition in high-stakes decisions is crucial until its accuracy and fairness can be demonstrably improved. These measures can help ensure that facial recognition technology is used responsibly and does not contribute to unjust outcomes.

The Boeing 737 MAX and its AI-driven Maneuvering Characteristics Augmentation System (MCAS) is a stark reminder of the potential catastrophic consequences of AI failures in safety-critical applications. The MCAS was designed to stabilize the aircraft by automatically adjusting the plane's nose position, but it relied on data from a single angle of attack sensor. When this sensor provided erroneous data, the system repeatedly forced the plane's nose down, contributing to two fatal crashes. The reasons for this failure include the reliance on a single point of failure; the system's dependence on data from only one sensor made it vulnerable to malfunctions. Additionally, there was a significant lack of pilot training and clear override mechanisms; pilots were not adequately trained on how to handle MCAS failures, and the system's automated responses were difficult to override. Finally, the system failed to undergo sufficient testing under extreme conditions and potential failure scenarios, leaving it vulnerable to catastrophic errors. To prevent such failures, it is critical to eliminate single points of failure in AI systems, particularly in safety-critical applications. Incorporating redundancy through multiple sensors and cross-checking data can help ensure system reliability. Moreover, prioritizing human factors by designing AI systems that complement, rather than override, human decision-making, and providing clear controls for human intervention are essential. Comprehensive testing under realistic and extreme conditions is also necessary to identify and mitigate potential failure modes before deployment.

## 4.6 Discussion

Let's take a moment to reflect on the real-world applications of AI in security that we've just explored. By thinking critically about these case studies, you can uncover valuable insights that might be relevant to your own organization's security efforts. Here are some questions to guide your reflection, helping you to draw practical lessons from these examples and consider how they could be adapted to fit your own needs.

First, think about what aspects of the AI implementations in these case studies could be adapted to your organization's cybersecurity needs. Are there specific techniques, like using machine learning for anomaly detection or employing natural language processing to scan communications, that could address challenges you're currently facing? Maybe the real-time monitoring and continuous learning aspects of these systems could be especially beneficial for your environment. Reflect on how these technologies could be tailored to fit your organization's unique requirements, helping to strengthen your security posture.

Next, consider the challenges faced in these implementations and how you might avoid or mitigate similar issues in your own setting. For example, many AI systems struggle with false positives, integration difficulties, or require high-quality data to function effectively. What steps could you take to overcome these hurdles? This might involve ensuring thorough data preprocessing, setting up robust pilot testing phases, or developing clear protocols for how AI systems interact with your existing security infrastructure. By anticipating these challenges early on, you can develop strategies to smooth the path for AI integration in your organization.

Finally, reflect on how the successes of these AI systems could inspire new initiatives or improvements in your own cybersecurity strategies. Perhaps the significant reduction in fraudulent transactions in the retail case, or the effective real-time anomaly detection in healthcare, sparks ideas for similar approaches in your environment. What new initiatives could you launch, or which existing strategies could be enhanced by applying the lessons learned from these case studies? Whether it's adopting a more proactive approach to threat detection, investing in AI-driven data analysis, or improving response times through automation, let these examples inspire you to think creatively about advancing your own security measures.

By engaging with these reflections, you're not just learning from other organizations' experiences—you're actively considering how to leverage AI to meet your specific cybersecurity challenges. This kind of critical thinking is key to staying ahead in the ever-evolving landscape of digital threats, enabling you to build a more resilient and adaptive security framework for your organization.

## 4.7 Learnings

Through these case studies, we've seen how AI and ML are revolutionizing cybersecurity across various sectors, demonstrating their ability to adapt to different environments, improve security measures, and address specific challenges. AI systems showcase remarkable adaptability, evolving with changing threat landscapes, which allows organizations to stay ahead of emerging risks. The importance of high-quality data is another critical takeaway, as the effectiveness of AI models depends heavily on the robustness of the data used for training. Furthermore, these examples emphasize the value of collaboration between AI experts and industry professionals, ensuring that security solutions are tailored to meet the unique needs of each sector. By reflecting on these practical applications, you can gain insights into the real-world potential of AI in cybersecurity and the practical steps needed to integrate these technologies into your own security strategies.

- AI's adaptability, data quality, and collaborative efforts are crucial for effective cybersecurity solutions.

# 5 Advanced Topics

**CONTENTS**

| | | |
|---|---|---|
| 5.1 | Introduction | 33 |
| 5.2 | Predictive Security: Anticipating Threats with AI | 34 |
| 5.3 | Adversarial AI: Understanding and Defending Against AI Exploits | 35 |
| 5.4 | AI in Encryption and Cryptography | 35 |
| 5.5 | Discussion | 36 |
| 5.6 | Learnings? | 37 |

## 5.1 Introduction

In this chapter, we venture into the cutting-edge world of AI and ML in cybersecurity, exploring advanced topics that are redefining the way security is approached and implemented. We'll dive into areas that push the boundaries of current technology, such as predictive security models, adversarial AI, and the application of AI in encryption and cryptography. These are not just theoretical concepts but are actively shaping the future landscape of cybersecurity, offering new tools and methods to address complex and evolving threats.By engaging with these advanced topics, you'll gain a deeper understanding of how AI is driving innovation in security. Predictive security models, for example, use AI to anticipate potential threats before they happen, allowing organizations to take proactive measures rather than merely reacting to attacks after they occur. This shift from reactive to predictive security represents a significant leap forward in how we defend against cyber threats, making systems not just smarter but also more resilient.

We'll also explore the realm of adversarial AI, which involves the use of AI to both attack and defend against other AI systems. This area is particularly relevant as malicious actors begin to harness AI for their own purposes, creating a new kind of arms race in cybersecurity. Understanding how adversarial AI works and how it can be countered is crucial for staying ahead in this rapidly evolving field.Finally, we'll look at how AI is being applied to encryption and cryptography, two foundational elements of digital security. AI is enhancing these processes by developing more robust encryption methods and finding vulnerabilities in existing systems, offering both new opportunities and challenges. As encryption becomes more sophisticated, so too does the need for advanced AI tools to keep pace with these developments.

Through this chapter, you'll not only expand your knowledge of the latest AI applications in cybersecurity but also prepare yourself for the future challenges and opportunities at the intersection of AI technology and security. This forward-looking approach will equip you with the insights needed to navigate the complex landscape of advanced cybersecurity threats, ensuring that your strategies are not only current but also capable of adapting to what's next.

## 5.2 Predictive Security: Anticipating Threats with AI

Predictive security is an innovative approach that leverages AI to foresee and address potential threats before they have a chance to cause harm. Unlike traditional security methods that react to incidents after they occur, predictive security takes a proactive stance, using AI-driven insights to anticipate where vulnerabilities might arise and which threats are most likely to be exploited. This approach combines historical data with real-time analysis, allowing organizations to identify potential risks early and take preventive measures.The implementation of predictive security involves deploying systems that integrate machine learning algorithms designed to spot patterns that signal future attacks. These algorithms sift through vast amounts of data from past security incidents, such as types of attacks, methods used, and points of entry, and correlate these findings with current network activities. By analyzing these trends, the systems can forecast potential threats, highlighting areas that might be targeted and suggesting where defenses need to be bolstered. For example, if the AI detects an increase in phishing attempts in similar organizations, it can alert security teams to strengthen their email filters and educate employees about the latest phishing tactics.

The benefits of predictive security are substantial. By anticipating threats, organizations can allocate their resources more strategically, focusing on shoring up defenses in areas identified as most vulnerable. This not only enhances the overall security posture but also reduces the impact of potential attacks by addressing weaknesses before they can be exploited. Moreover, predictive security models shift the role of security teams from constantly reacting to breaches to taking proactive steps to prevent them. This proactive approach not only saves time and resources but also provides a significant strategic advantage, enabling organizations to stay one step ahead of cybercriminals. In

*Advanced Topics* 35

an environment where the threat landscape is continually evolving, the ability to predict and preemptively address risks is a game-changer, transforming how security is managed and significantly enhancing protection against cyber threats.

## 5.3 Adversarial AI: Understanding and Defending Against AI Exploits

Adversarial AI refers to techniques designed to deceive machine learning models by feeding them deliberately misleading data. This is a significant concern in cybersecurity, as malicious actors can exploit these vulnerabilities to bypass AI-driven security measures. For example, an adversarial attack might involve subtly altering the inputs that an AI system relies on—like tweaking the pixels in an image or modifying the structure of a data point—so that the AI misinterprets what it's seeing or analyzing. These kinds of attacks can be used to trick security systems into ignoring threats or allowing unauthorized access. To combat this, security researchers and AI developers are collaborating to build more resilient AI systems capable of withstanding adversarial attacks. A key strategy in this effort is known as adversarial training, where AI models are specifically trained on examples of adversarial inputs. This process involves repeatedly exposing the model to altered data that could potentially deceive it, allowing the model to learn and adapt so it becomes more resistant to such exploits. Other techniques include developing algorithms that can detect when data inputs have been tampered with or creating models that can self-adjust in real-time to counteract any manipulations. The benefits of defending against adversarial AI are far-reaching. By enhancing the robustness of AI systems, we ensure that they remain reliable and trustworthy, especially in critical applications like healthcare, finance, or national security, where mistakes can have severe consequences. Additionally, strengthening AI defenses against adversarial attacks not only protects the AI systems themselves but also reinforces the overall security framework they support. This ongoing battle between adversarial exploits and AI defenses continually pushes the boundaries of what AI can achieve in security, driving innovation and leading to the development of more sophisticated and resilient technologies. As AI becomes increasingly integrated into all aspects of security, ensuring that these systems can defend against adversarial threats is essential for maintaining the integrity and effectiveness of AI-driven solutions.

## 5.4 AI in Encryption and Cryptography

AI is revolutionizing the field of encryption and cryptography by automating complex processes and enhancing the security of data transmission and storage. Traditionally, cryptography has relied on human-designed algorithms and protocols to protect information, but AI brings a new level of sophistication to these tasks. By leveraging machine learning and other AI techniques, cryptographic processes can become more efficient, adaptive, and resilient against evolving threats.

One of the key ways AI is being implemented in this field is through the development of new cryptographic methods and the optimization of existing ones. For example, AI algorithms can be used to generate truly random keys for encryption, which are far more secure than those generated by traditional means. Randomness is a critical component of strong encryption, and AI's ability to produce high-quality random keys can significantly enhance the robustness of cryptographic systems. Additionally, AI can streamline the encryption process itself, making it faster and more efficient without sacrificing security. This is particularly important as the volume of data requiring encryption continues to grow, necessitating solutions that can keep up with the demand.

The benefits of AI-driven cryptography are substantial. By automating and refining encryption techniques, AI helps create more secure communication channels, ensuring that sensitive information remains protected from unauthorized access. This is crucial in sectors like finance, healthcare, and government, where the confidentiality and integrity of data are paramount. Furthermore, as encryption technologies continue to evolve, AI will play an increasingly vital role in staying ahead of new vulnerabilities and threats. It can rapidly adapt to changes in the threat landscape, providing a dynamic defense that traditional cryptographic methods cannot match.

Overall, the integration of AI into encryption and cryptography represents a significant advancement in data security. It not only improves the efficiency and effectiveness of these protective measures but also ensures that encryption can evolve alongside emerging challenges. As we continue to rely more heavily on digital communication and data storage, AI's role in maintaining secure and trustworthy encryption will be more important than ever, safeguarding the privacy and integrity of information in an increasingly interconnected world.

*Advanced Topics* 37

## 5.5 Discussion

To further explore the advanced topics of AI in cybersecurity, let's dive into some key discussion points that can help you think about how these technologies might apply within your own organization. Reflecting on these questions can deepen your understanding and inspire practical steps toward integrating these innovative solutions into your security strategies.First, think about **how predictive security models could be applied within your organization** to improve threat anticipation and prevention. Consider the specific areas where being able to predict threats before they occur would be most valuable. For instance, could predictive models help in identifying potential cyberattacks based on past incidents, or might they be used to forecast vulnerabilities in your network infrastructure? Reflect on the types of data you currently have access to and how this data could be utilized to build predictive models that provide actionable insights, allowing your security team to proactively address risks rather than just reacting to them.

Next, consider what steps your organization can take to protect its AI systems from adversarial attacks. As adversarial AI becomes more sophisticated, it's crucial to think about the vulnerabilities your AI-driven tools might have and how to safeguard them. What strategies could you implement to harden your AI systems against manipulative inputs or deceptive data? This might include adversarial training, regular audits of AI models, or setting up monitoring systems to detect unusual behavior that could indicate an attack. Reflect on how these defenses can be integrated into your existing security framework to ensure that your AI systems remain reliable and effective.

Finally, reflect on how AI-enhanced encryption could benefit your current security protocols. Consider the role of encryption in your organization's data protection strategy and how AI could take it to the next level. Could AI-driven encryption methods improve the speed and efficiency of your data encryption processes, or perhaps offer stronger protection through more advanced key generation techniques? Think about the specific security challenges you face with data transmission and storage, and how AI could address these challenges by making your encryption methods more robust and adaptive.

Engaging with these questions not only helps you explore the potential of advanced AI concepts in cybersecurity but also encourages you to think critically about how these innovations can be practically applied in your own environment. By considering how predictive models, adversarial defenses, and AI-enhanced encryption could fit into your organization, you're taking important steps toward leveraging AI to create a more secure, resilient, and forward-thinking security strategy.

## 5.6 Learnings?

This chapter has introduced us to some of the most advanced and innovative applications of AI in cybersecurity, highlighting the transformative potential of these technologies. From predictive security models that shift cybersecurity from a reactive to a proactive discipline, to understanding the importance of resilience against adversarial AI, and exploring AI's role in revolutionizing encryption and cryptography, we've gained valuable insights into the future of cybersecurity. As we conclude, it's essential to remember that these topics are not just theoretical; they represent practical opportunities to enhance security strategies, making them more proactive, resilient, and aligned with the latest advancements in AI. Let these insights inspire you to adopt advanced AI solutions, ensuring your organization's security measures are prepared for the challenges of tomorrow.

- Predictive security models can transform cybersecurity from reactive to proactive.

- Resilience against adversarial AI is crucial for robust AI systems.

- AI-driven encryption has the potential to revolutionize data protection.

- Advanced AI applications enable more adaptive and intelligent security measures.

- Future-ready cybersecurity requires integrating the latest AI advancements.

# 6

## Ethical and Legal Considerations

**CONTENTS**

| | | |
|---|---|---|
| 6.1 | Introduction | 39 |
| 6.2 | Balancing Security Needs with Privacy Rights | 40 |
| | 6.2.1 Discussion Points: | 40 |
| 6.3 | Ethical AI Use in Surveillance and Monitoring | 41 |
| | 6.3.1 Discussion Points: | 41 |
| 6.4 | Interactive Discussion: Navigating Ethical and Legal Terrain | 41 |
| | 6.4.1 Discussion Points: | 42 |
| 6.5 | Key Learnings and Reflections | 42 |

## 6.1 Introduction

As we explore the ethical and legal landscapes surrounding the deployment of AI and ML technologies in cybersecurity, Chapter 6 takes a closer look at the responsibilities and challenges that professionals in the field must navigate. This chapter is crafted to help you understand the intricate maze of ethical dilemmas and regulatory frameworks that come into play when implementing AI-driven security solutions. It's not just about making systems smarter or more efficient; it's also about ensuring that your practices enhance security while upholding the highest standards of integrity and legality.In this chapter, you'll gain insights into the ethical considerations that accompany the use of AI in cybersecurity, such as the potential for biases in AI models, the implications of automated decision-making, and the privacy concerns that arise when analyzing large sets of personal data. We'll discuss the importance of transparency, accountability, and fairness in AI applications, emphasizing the need for professionals to consider the broader impact of their technologies on individuals and society.

Additionally, we'll navigate the regulatory landscape, exploring the various laws and guidelines that govern the use of AI in security contexts. From data protection regulations to specific AI-related standards, understanding these frameworks is crucial for ensuring that your implementations comply with legal requirements and ethical norms. The goal of this chapter is to equip you with the knowledge and tools needed to make informed decisions that align with both your organizational objectives and the broader societal expectations of responsible AI use.By delving into these topics, you'll be better prepared to face the ethical and legal challenges inherent in deploying AI and ML in cybersecurity. This chapter serves as a guide to not only help you avoid potential pitfalls but also to inspire confidence in your ability to implement AI solutions that are both effective and ethically sound. As you work to enhance security, this chapter reminds us that the integrity of our methods is just as important as the results they achieve.

## 6.2 Balancing Security Needs with Privacy Rights

The integration of AI into cybersecurity often brings up significant privacy concerns, especially when it comes to data collection and surveillance capabilities. Striking the right balance between enhancing security and respecting individual privacy rights is essential. This section delves into the challenges and strategies for achieving this balance.

### 6.2.1 Discussion Points:

It's important to evaluate whether the AI systems being deployed are truly necessary for achieving the security goals they are intended to support. Consider whether the level of intrusion into personal privacy is proportional to the security benefits gained. This involves a careful analysis of the data being collected, the potential impact on individuals' privacy, and whether the same security objectives could be met with less intrusive methods. By assessing necessity and proportionality, organizations can ensure that their use of AI in security does not overreach and respects the fundamental rights of individuals.

To mitigate privacy risks while still benefiting from AI-driven security measures, it is essential to explore Privacy-Enhancing Technologies (PETs). These technologies, such as data anonymization, differential privacy, and encryption, allow organizations to protect sensitive information while analyzing data for security purposes. For instance, anonymizing personal data before processing can help minimize the risk of identifying individuals while still allowing AI systems to detect patterns and threats. Encryption ensures that data remains secure even if intercepted. By integrating PETs, organizations can strike a balance between robust security measures and the protection of individual privacy rights, thus building trust and compliance with legal standards.Balancing the need for security with the preservation of privacy rights is a complex but critical task. By carefully assessing the necessity and propor-

*Ethical and Legal Considerations* 41

tionality of AI systems and incorporating Privacy-Enhancing Technologies, organizations can navigate these challenges effectively, ensuring that their security practices uphold ethical standards and respect individual privacy.

## 6.3 Ethical AI Use in Surveillance and Monitoring

**Overview:** The deployment of AI in surveillance and monitoring, particularly by state authorities or large corporations, raises substantial ethical concerns. These concerns include issues of consent, transparency, and accountability. When AI is used to monitor individuals, it can infringe on privacy and autonomy, leading to a need for clear guidelines and ethical considerations to ensure responsible use.

### 6.3.1 Discussion Points:

One of the critical challenges in ethical AI use for surveillance is ensuring that individuals are adequately informed about monitoring practices and have given their consent. Organizations must consider how to communicate the scope and purpose of surveillance clearly, allowing individuals to understand how their data is being used. This might include providing accessible privacy notices, offering opt-in options, and ensuring that individuals are aware of their rights. Transparency is key to maintaining trust, so organizations should aim to disclose the technologies and data involved in their surveillance activities in an open and understandable manner.

Establishing accountability is essential for the ethical use of AI in surveillance. This involves creating mechanisms that hold entities responsible for how AI systems are deployed and operated. Accountability measures could include regular audits of AI systems to check for compliance with ethical standards, the implementation of oversight bodies to monitor AI use, and the creation of clear policies outlining acceptable use cases and consequences for misuse. Additionally, there should be avenues for individuals to report concerns or abuses related to AI-driven surveillance, ensuring that there are checks and balances to prevent overreach and protect individual rights.The ethical use of AI in surveillance and monitoring requires a careful balance between security needs and the rights of individuals. By prioritizing consent, transparency, and robust accountability mechanisms, organizations can help ensure that their surveillance practices respect ethical standards and build public trust in their AI systems.

## 6.4 Interactive Discussion: Navigating Ethical and Legal Terrain

Engage with the following questions to critically reflect on how your organization can navigate the complex ethical and legal considerations surrounding the use of AI in cybersecurity and surveillance. These reflections are designed to help you develop strategies that balance security needs with the protection of individual rights.

### 6.4.1 Discussion Points:

What steps can be taken to ensure that AI systems in your organization respect privacy rights while maintaining security effectiveness? Consider implementing privacy-by-design principles, which involve incorporating privacy considerations into the development and deployment of AI systems from the outset. This might include minimizing data collection, anonymizing data wherever possible, and ensuring that access to sensitive information is strictly controlled. Additionally, regular privacy impact assessments can help identify and mitigate risks to individual privacy.How can your organization stay informed and compliant with the latest AI regulations affecting cybersecurity? Keeping up with evolving legal standards and regulations is crucial. Organizations should establish a dedicated team or appoint a compliance officer responsible for monitoring regulatory changes related to AI and cybersecurity. This team can also develop training programs to educate employees about the legal obligations associated with AI use, ensuring that all practices align with current laws and best practices.What ethical guidelines should be established to govern the use of AI in surveillance within your organization? Developing a clear set of ethical guidelines is essential for responsible AI use. These guidelines should address key issues such as consent, data minimization, and the purpose of surveillance activities. Organizations might consider setting up an ethics committee to review and oversee AI surveillance projects, ensuring that they align with ethical standards and societal values. Establishing a transparent decision-making process and providing avenues for stakeholders to voice concerns can also enhance accountability and trust.

Navigating the ethical and legal landscape of AI in cybersecurity requires a proactive approach that prioritizes respect for individual rights and compliance with regulations. By engaging with these questions, your organization can develop robust strategies to address these challenges, ensuring that AI technologies are used responsibly and effectively.

## 6.5 Key Learnings and Reflections

This chapter has emphasized the critical need to integrate ethical considerations and legal requirements when deploying AI and ML in cybersecurity. Understanding that these factors are not just secondary concerns but central to the responsible use of AI helps ensure that technologies are implemented in a way that respects both human rights and regulatory standards. As we move forward, it's important to keep these insights at the forefront of your AI strategies, using them as a guide to maintain compliance and uphold ethical integrity.

- Balancing security advancements with individual rights is crucial for sustainable AI deployment.

- Navigating complex regulations is essential to avoid legal repercussions and maintain trust.

- Establishing ethical governance frameworks ensures responsible AI use with transparency and accountability.

- Integrating privacy-by-design principles helps safeguard individual privacy while achieving security goals.

- Staying informed and engaged with regulatory changes enables organizations to adapt and comply effectively.

# 7
# Regulations and Compliance in AI Security

## CONTENTS

| | | | |
|---|---|---|---|
| 7.1 | Introduction | | 45 |
| 7.2 | The Growing Importance of AI Regulation | | 46 |
| | 7.2.1 | Key Regulations Affecting AI in Security | 46 |
| | | 7.2.1.1 General Data Protection Regulation (GDPR) | 46 |
| | | 7.2.1.2 California Consumer Privacy Act (CCPA) | 47 |
| | | 7.2.1.3 AI Act (European Union) | 47 |
| | | 7.2.1.4 National AI Initiative Act (United States) | 47 |
| | | 7.2.1.5 Sector-Specific Regulations | 48 |
| 7.3 | Emerging Trends in AI Regulation | | 48 |
| 7.4 | Discussion | | 50 |
| 7.5 | Learnings? | | 50 |

## 7.1 Introduction

As artificial intelligence (AI) continues to revolutionize the security landscape, the legal and regulatory frameworks governing its use are evolving at a rapid pace. The deployment of AI in security offers tremendous potential, from enhancing threat detection to automating responses to cyberattacks. However, this promise comes with significant legal and ethical considerations. Organizations utilizing AI for security purposes must navigate a complex and ever-changing landscape of regulations designed to balance the need for technological innovation with the protection of individual rights, privacy, and broader societal values.

These regulations vary widely by region and jurisdiction, reflecting differing societal norms and legislative priorities. In many cases, laws are being developed to address concerns such as data privacy, algorithmic transparency, and accountability in AI-driven decision-making. For example, the European Union's General Data Protection Regulation (GDPR) has set a high bar for data privacy standards, influencing global practices even beyond its borders.

Meanwhile, emerging regulations, like the proposed AI Act in the EU, are aiming to establish frameworks specifically addressing the risks associated with AI applications, including those in security.

For organizations leveraging AI in security, staying compliant is not merely a matter of checking boxes; it requires a proactive approach to understanding and integrating regulatory requirements into the development and deployment of AI systems. This includes conducting regular audits, maintaining clear documentation of AI models and their decision-making processes, and implementing robust data governance practices. For security professionals, business leaders, and developers alike, grasping the nuances of these regulations is crucial not only for avoiding legal pitfalls but also for fostering public trust and ensuring that AI technologies are used responsibly and ethically. As the regulatory landscape continues to evolve, staying informed and adaptable will be key to successfully navigating the challenges and opportunities that AI in security presents.

## 7.2 The Growing Importance of AI Regulation

Artificial intelligence in security offers remarkable benefits, such as enhancing threat detection, streamlining incident response, and automating routine security tasks. However, the power of AI comes with significant responsibilities. As AI becomes more embedded in security practices, governments and regulatory bodies worldwide are increasingly attentive to the potential risks it poses, including privacy infringements, algorithmic bias, and unforeseen consequences. These concerns have led to the establishment of various regulations aimed at ensuring that AI technologies are deployed ethically, transparently, and safely. The goal of these regulations is not to stifle innovation but to create a framework that promotes responsible use of AI, protecting individual rights and maintaining societal trust. As the landscape of AI regulation continues to evolve, organizations must stay ahead of these changes to avoid legal pitfalls and align with best practices.

### 7.2.1 Key Regulations Affecting AI in Security

"nobreak

#### 7.2.1.1 General Data Protection Regulation (GDPR)

The GDPR is one of the most stringent and comprehensive data protection laws globally, and it has a significant impact on AI applications in security. Under the GDPR, any AI system that processes personal data must comply with rigorous requirements regarding data collection, processing, and storage.

Organizations are obligated to obtain explicit consent from individuals before collecting their data, and the data must only be used for the purposes that have been clearly communicated and agreed upon. Additionally, the GDPR emphasizes the rights of individuals to access, correct, or delete their data, and mandates that organizations implement strong security measures to protect personal data from unauthorized access or breaches. **Compliance Tip**: To reduce the risk of non-compliance, organizations should adopt data minimization practices, ensuring that only the necessary data is collected and used. Implementing anonymization techniques can also help in safeguarding personal data. Regularly auditing AI models is essential to verify that they are not processing data in ways that contravene GDPR requirements, thereby maintaining compliance and protecting individuals' privacy rights.

### 7.2.1.2 California Consumer Privacy Act (CCPA)

The CCPA represents one of the most robust state-level privacy laws in the United States, focusing on the privacy rights of consumers, particularly in California. Similar to the GDPR, the CCPA grants individuals the right to know what personal data is being collected about them, how it is being used, and with whom it is shared. It also provides consumers the right to request the deletion of their personal data and to opt out of its sale. For AI systems in security, this means implementing mechanisms that allow consumers to easily exercise these rights, such as user-friendly interfaces for data access and deletion requests. **Compliance Tip**: Organizations should ensure they provide clear, accessible privacy notices that outline how their AI systems collect and use data. It is crucial to implement robust mechanisms that allow consumers to easily exercise their rights under the CCPA, such as straightforward processes for accessing, correcting, or deleting their personal data.

### 7.2.1.3 AI Act (European Union)

The proposed AI Act by the European Union is a pioneering legislative framework that categorizes AI systems based on their risk levels: unacceptable, high, limited, and minimal. Security-related AI applications, which often fall under the high-risk category, will be subject to stringent regulations. These include mandatory risk assessments, transparency obligations, and requirements for human oversight to ensure that AI systems operate in a manner that is safe, ethical, and accountable. The AI Act is poised to set a global standard for AI governance, influencing how AI systems are developed and deployed not only within Europe but also worldwide. **Compliance Tip**: Organizations should conduct comprehensive risk assessments of their AI applications to determine their classification under the AI Act. For high-risk AI systems, it is crucial to establish processes for continuous monitoring and human oversight, ensuring that these systems remain aligned with regulatory requirements and ethical standards.

### 7.2.1.4 National AI Initiative Act (United States)

While the National AI Initiative Act is not a regulatory framework in the strictest sense, it outlines a national strategy for promoting the responsible development and use of AI in the United States. The act emphasizes the need for AI systems to be transparent, explainable, and secure, and it supports the development of standards and guidelines to achieve these goals. A key component of this initiative is the involvement of the National Institute of Standards and Technology (NIST), which has developed guidelines that stress the importance of explainability, fairness, and robustness in AI systems. **Compliance Tip**: To align with the principles outlined in the National AI Initiative Act, organizations should follow NIST's guidelines when developing AI systems for security. This includes incorporating features that enhance the transparency and explainability of AI models, ensuring that they operate in a fair and unbiased manner, and implementing robust security measures to protect against vulnerabilities and attacks.

### 7.2.1.5 Sector-Specific Regulations

In addition to general AI regulations, various industries have specific laws and standards that impact AI applications in security. For example, in the healthcare sector, the Health Insurance Portability and Accountability Act (HIPAA) governs the use of AI to ensure that patient data is protected. Similarly, the Federal Trade Commission (FTC) oversees AI applications in consumer protection, ensuring that AI systems do not engage in deceptive or unfair practices. Organizations deploying AI in these sectors must be vigilant in understanding and complying with the relevant regulations that apply to their specific industry. **Compliance Tip**: It is essential for organizations to identify the sector-specific regulations that apply to their operations and ensure that their AI systems are fully compliant with these standards. For instance, in healthcare, this might involve implementing robust data protection measures to ensure that AI-driven security tools safeguard patient information in accordance with HIPAA requirements. Regularly updating compliance practices to reflect changes in regulations is also crucial for maintaining adherence to these legal frameworks.

## 7.3 Emerging Trends in AI Regulation

As AI technology continues to evolve at a rapid pace, so too do the regulations that seek to govern its use. These regulations are not just reactive measures; they are increasingly proactive efforts to address the complex and multifaceted challenges that AI presents. A number of key trends are emerging as regulators and policymakers around the world grapple with the implications of AI, particularly in critical areas like security. These trends reflect a broader understanding that the ethical, transparent, and accountable use of AI is essential to safeguarding public trust and ensuring that AI technologies are used for the greater good.

One of the most significant emerging trends in AI regulation is the emphasis on algorithmic accountability. Regulators are increasingly demanding that organizations take responsibility for the decisions made by their AI models, particularly in high-stakes domains such as security. This trend is driven by the recognition that AI algorithms can have profound impacts on individuals and society, and that these impacts must be managed with care. Algorithmic accountability involves several key components, including the need for transparency in how AI models make decisions, the ability to audit and explain these decisions, and the establishment of clear lines of responsibility when AI systems fail or produce unintended outcomes. This push for accountability is not just about compliance; it is about building systems that are trustworthy and that operate in ways that align with societal values.

Alongside algorithmic accountability, there is a growing focus on the ethical use of AI. New standards and frameworks are being developed to guide organizations in implementing AI in ways that are fair, transparent, and free from bias. These ethical guidelines emphasize the importance of designing AI systems that do not perpetuate or exacerbate existing inequalities, and that respect the rights and dignity of all individuals. This includes considerations around data privacy, informed consent, and the right to explanation, especially in contexts where AI-driven decisions can have significant consequences. By embedding ethical considerations into the core of AI development and deployment, regulators aim to ensure that AI serves as a force for good, rather than a source of harm or discrimination.

Another critical trend in AI regulation is the push for global coordination and cooperation. AI is a borderless technology, and its impacts are felt across national boundaries. As a result, there is a growing recognition that effective regulation cannot occur in isolation. Countries are increasingly engaging in international dialogues to align their regulatory approaches and to develop harmonized standards that can apply globally. This trend towards global coordination seeks to prevent a patchwork of conflicting regulations that could stifle innovation or allow AI systems developed in one jurisdiction to bypass the rules in another. By working together, nations aim to create a more consistent and cohesive regulatory landscape that supports the safe and responsible use of AI worldwide.

These emerging trends reflect a broader shift towards a more mature and considered approach to AI regulation. As AI continues to play an increasingly central role in security and other critical areas, staying ahead of these regulatory trends will be essential for organizations that wish to leverage AI responsibly and effectively. By embracing algorithmic accountability, adhering to ethical AI standards, and participating in global regulatory initiatives, organizations can not only ensure compliance but also contribute to the development of AI systems that are aligned with the broader values and expectations of society.

## 7.4 Discussion

As we delve into the evolving landscape of AI regulation, it's clear that the intersection of technology, ethics, and law is becoming increasingly complex and critical to navigate. The push for algorithmic accountability highlights the need for transparency and responsibility in AI, especially in high-stakes sectors like security where decisions can have far-reaching consequences. This discussion invites us to consider not just the technical aspects of AI, but also the broader societal implications. Are we doing enough to ensure that AI systems are not just efficient, but also fair and trustworthy? The rise of ethical AI standards challenges developers and organizations to move beyond mere compliance and to actively design systems that respect human rights and minimize biases. Moreover, the trend towards global coordination underscores that AI regulation cannot be confined within national borders; it requires a unified approach that addresses the global nature of AI technologies. These trends invite us to think critically about our role as developers, business leaders, or policy makers in shaping a future where AI contributes positively to society without compromising individual rights and ethical standards.

## 7.5 Learnings?

In this chapter, we explored the dynamic and rapidly evolving world of AI regulation, emphasizing the importance of accountability, ethical standards, and global cooperation. The key takeaway is that while AI offers immense potential, its deployment comes with significant responsibilities that cannot be overlooked. Understanding and navigating these regulations is essential for ensuring that AI technologies are used in ways that are safe, transparent, and aligned with societal values. By delving into various regulations like GDPR, CCPA, and the proposed AI Act, it becomes clear that compliance is not just a legal requirement but a fundamental component of responsible AI development. This chapter underscored the importance of staying informed and proactive in adapting to regulatory changes, and highlighted the critical role of ethical considerations in guiding the development and implementation of AI systems.

# 8
## AI and IoT Security

**CONTENTS**

- 8.1 Introduction .................................................................. 51
- 8.2 The Unique Challenges of IoT Security ........................ 52
  - 8.2.1 Diverse and Fragmented Ecosystem ................ 52
    - 8.2.1.1 Limited Processing Power and Storage ...... 53
  - Scalability and Communication ................................. 53
  - Lack of Standardization ............................................ 53
  - How AI Enhances IoT Security ................................. 54
  - Anomaly Detection .................................................... 54
  - Predictive Maintenance and Threat Forecasting ....... 54
  - Automated Threat Response ..................................... 54
  - Behavioral Biometrics ............................................... 55
  - Enhanced Data Security ............................................ 55
- 8.3 Practical Solutions for Securing IoT with AI ............... 55
  - 8.3.1 Deploy AI-Driven Security Gateways ............. 55
  - 8.3.2 Use Lightweight AI Models .............................. 56
  - 8.3.3 Adopt Edge AI for Real-Time Security ........... 56
  - 8.3.4 Implement Continuous Learning and Adaptation ....... 56
  - 8.3.5 Integrate AI with Existing Security Frameworks ....... 56
- 8.4 Challenges of Implementing AI in IoT Security ........... 57
  - 8.4.1 Data Privacy Concerns ..................................... 57
- 8.5 Learning? ...................................................................... 57

## 8.1 Introduction

The Internet of Things (IoT) has revolutionized the way we interact with technology, embedding connectivity into a vast array of everyday objects—from smart home devices like thermostats and lighting systems to wearable fitness trackers, industrial sensors, and even critical medical equipment. This interconnected network of devices has transformed industries, driven efficiencies, and enhanced the convenience of daily life. However, as IoT adoption continues to grow at an unprecedented pace, so too does the attack surface for potential cyber threats. With billions of connected devices generating and transmitting vast amounts of data, the challenge of ensuring IoT security has become a critical concern for businesses, governments, and consumers alike. The sheer volume of devices, coupled with their diversity and varying levels of security, creates numerous vulnerabilities that cybercriminals can exploit. This chapter explores how artificial intelligence (AI) can be leveraged to enhance IoT security by addressing the unique challenges posed by these interconnected devices. By examining the current landscape of IoT security, identifying the specific challenges, and presenting AI-driven solutions, this chapter aims to provide a comprehensive understanding of how AI can be instrumental in safeguarding IoT environments against evolving cyber threats.

## 8.2 The Unique Challenges of IoT Security

The security of IoT devices is uniquely challenging due to their inherent characteristics. IoT devices are often designed to be small, efficient, and specialized for specific tasks, which means they are usually resource-constrained with limited processing power, memory, and storage capabilities. Unlike traditional computing devices, many IoT devices do not have the capacity to support comprehensive security measures like traditional endpoint security solutions. Furthermore, the IoT landscape is highly fragmented and diverse, encompassing a wide range of devices from different manufacturers, each with its own set of standards, protocols, and security practices. This lack of uniformity complicates the implementation of a one-size-fits-all security solution, making it difficult to standardize protections across the entire ecosystem.

Another critical challenge is the scalability of IoT security. As the number of connected devices continues to grow exponentially, managing and securing these devices at scale becomes increasingly complex. Manual monitoring and intervention are not practical in large-scale IoT deployments, necessitating automated, scalable security solutions that can adapt to the growing landscape. Additionally, many IoT devices communicate over unsecure networks or through unencrypted channels, making them susceptible to various forms of cyberattacks, such as interception, spoofing, and data manipulation. The lack of standardized security protocols further exacerbates these vulnerabilities, as security implementations vary widely across devices, leading to inconsistent protection levels and increased risks.

### 8.2.1 Diverse and Fragmented Ecosystem

The IoT ecosystem is characterized by its diversity and fragmentation. It includes a vast array of devices, from simple sensors that monitor environmental conditions to complex machinery used in industrial settings. Each of these devices may come from different manufacturers and operate under different standards and protocols. This diversity makes it exceedingly difficult to develop a unified security strategy that can be applied across all IoT devices. The fragmented nature of the ecosystem also means that vulnerabilities in one type of device can differ significantly from those in another, requiring tailored security solutions that can address specific threats.

#### 8.2.1.1 Limited Processing Power and Storage

Many IoT devices are designed with minimal processing power, limited memory, and constrained storage capacities. These limitations pose significant challenges when it comes to implementing traditional security measures, such as encryption, intrusion detection systems, or regular software updates. In many cases, the hardware constraints of IoT devices prevent them from running complex security protocols or from being updated regularly, which can leave them vulnerable to known security threats.

### Scalability and Communication

The scalability of IoT security is another major challenge. With billions of devices expected to be connected to the internet in the coming years, managing security across such a vast network is a daunting task. The sheer volume of data generated by IoT devices also complicates the security landscape, as traditional security monitoring and management tools may not be equipped to handle the massive scale and real-time nature of IoT data. Automated, AI-driven security solutions are essential to managing the scale of IoT deployments, enabling real-time detection and response to potential threats.

IoT devices often rely on wireless communication protocols, such as Wi-Fi, Bluetooth, or Zigbee, to connect with other devices and networks. These communication channels are not always secure, and in many cases, they lack robust encryption or authentication mechanisms. This makes IoT devices particularly vulnerable to attacks that exploit these unsecure communication channels, such as eavesdropping, spoofing, and data interception.

### Lack of Standardization

The lack of standardized security protocols across the IoT landscape further complicates the security of these devices. Without consistent standards, manufacturers implement varying levels of security, leading to a wide disparity in how well different devices are protected. This inconsistency can create weak points in an otherwise secure network, as attackers often target the least secure devices to gain entry into the broader system.

## How AI Enhances IoT Security

Artificial intelligence offers a powerful set of tools to address the unique security challenges posed by IoT environments. By leveraging machine learning, pattern recognition, and advanced data analytics, AI can provide dynamic, scalable, and effective security solutions tailored specifically to the needs of IoT. AI can enhance IoT security in several key ways, including anomaly detection, predictive maintenance, automated threat response, behavioral biometrics, and enhanced data security. Each of these applications allows for more intelligent, adaptive, and proactive security measures that can better protect IoT devices from evolving cyber threats.

### Anomaly Detection

AI algorithms excel at detecting patterns and identifying deviations from the norm, making them particularly well-suited for anomaly detection in IoT environments. Machine learning models can be trained to recognize the normal behavior patterns of IoT devices, such as typical traffic flows, access times, and usage patterns. When these models detect deviations from the established norms—such as unusual traffic patterns, unauthorized access attempts, or abnormal device behavior—they can flag these anomalies as potential security threats in real-time. For instance, if a smart thermostat suddenly starts communicating with an unfamiliar IP address, an AI-driven anomaly detection system can quickly identify this as a potential botnet attempt and alert the security team or take automated actions to mitigate the risk.

### Predictive Maintenance and Threat Forecasting

AI's predictive capabilities extend beyond immediate threat detection to include forecasting potential vulnerabilities or failures before they occur. By analyzing historical data from IoT devices, AI can predict when a device is likely to fail or become susceptible to attacks, allowing for preemptive maintenance or security updates. This proactive approach helps to mitigate risks before they can be exploited by attackers. For example, in an industrial IoT setup, AI can analyze patterns of device performance and environmental conditions to predict when a sensor is likely to malfunction or be targeted by a cyberattack, enabling timely intervention and reducing downtime or damage.

### Automated Threat Response

One of the most powerful applications of AI in IoT security is the automation of threat responses. When a security breach or anomaly is detected, AI systems can automatically initiate responses such as isolating compromised devices, blocking suspicious IP addresses, applying security patches, or even shutting down affected devices. This rapid response capability significantly reduces the time between threat detection and mitigation, limiting the potential damage caused by cyberattacks. For example, in the event of a Distributed Denial of Service (DDoS) attack originating from multiple IoT devices, an AI system can quickly reroute traffic, block the offending IPs, and alert the security team, all within seconds of detecting the attack.

**Behavioral Biometrics**

AI can also enhance IoT security through the use of behavioral biometrics, which involves analyzing patterns of behavior to authenticate users and detect unauthorized access attempts. Behavioral biometrics can include factors such as device usage patterns, physical movements, or even the unique ways in which a user interacts with a device. By incorporating these biometric factors into security protocols, AI can add an additional layer of protection that goes beyond traditional password-based authentication. For example, a smart lock might use AI to recognize the unique way an authorized user approaches and interacts with it, denying access if a different pattern is detected, thereby preventing unauthorized entry.

**Enhanced Data Security**

AI-driven algorithms can continuously monitor data flows within IoT environments, identifying and mitigating potential vulnerabilities in real-time. This includes securing data both at rest and in transit, using advanced encryption techniques that are optimized for the limited processing capabilities of many IoT devices. For instance, AI can detect when sensitive data, such as health information from a wearable device, is being transmitted over an insecure channel and can automatically initiate encryption protocols to protect the data. This proactive approach ensures that data remains secure, even when transmitted across potentially vulnerable networks.

## 8.3 Practical Solutions for Securing IoT with AI

To effectively leverage AI for IoT security, organizations must adopt practical solutions that are tailored to the specific needs and constraints of their IoT environments. This includes deploying AI-driven security gateways, using lightweight AI models, adopting edge AI for real-time security, implementing continuous learning and adaptation, and integrating AI with existing security frameworks.

### 8.3.1 Deploy AI-Driven Security Gateways

AI-driven security gateways serve as a centralized point of control and protection for IoT devices. These gateways sit between IoT devices and the internet, monitoring traffic, detecting anomalies, and enforcing security policies that are specifically tailored to IoT environments. By centralizing security functions, AI-driven gateways reduce the burden on individual devices, ensuring consistent security enforcement across the network. This approach also allows for more sophisticated threat detection and response capabilities, leveraging the full processing power of AI without overwhelming the limited resources of individual IoT devices.

### 8.3.2 Use Lightweight AI Models

For resource-constrained IoT devices, deploying lightweight AI models that can run on limited hardware is essential. These models are designed to provide essential security functions, such as anomaly detection and basic threat response, without consuming excessive processing power or memory. By optimizing AI algorithms for efficiency, even the smallest IoT devices can benefit from intelligent security measures that are appropriate for their capabilities, ensuring that no device is left unprotected due to resource limitations.

### 8.3.3 Adopt Edge AI for Real-Time Security

Edge AI brings processing power closer to the IoT devices, enabling real-time threat detection and response. By processing data locally at the edge of the network rather than sending it to a central server, edge AI reduces latency, enhances privacy, and provides immediate, localized protection for IoT devices. This approach is particularly beneficial in scenarios where rapid response times are critical, such as in industrial automation or healthcare applications, where delays in threat detection and response could have significant consequences.

### 8.3.4 Implement Continuous Learning and Adaptation

AI models used in IoT security should be designed with the capability to learn and adapt over time. This continuous learning allows the models to improve their detection accuracy and effectiveness as new threats emerge. By incorporating mechanisms for dynamic learning and adaptation, AI systems can keep pace with the ever-evolving threat landscape, enhancing the resilience and robustness of IoT security measures.

### 8.3.5 Integrate AI with Existing Security Frameworks

To maximize the effectiveness of AI in IoT security, it should be integrated with existing security frameworks and protocols. This layered approach combines the strengths of AI with traditional security measures, such as firewalls, intrusion detection systems, and anti-virus software, providing comprehensive protection for IoT environments. By complementing existing security infrastructure, AI can enhance the overall security posture of IoT deployments, ensuring that all potential vulnerabilities are addressed.

## 8.4 Challenges of Implementing AI in IoT Security

While AI offers powerful solutions for enhancing IoT security, its implementation is not without challenges. Key issues include data privacy concerns, high initial costs, and the complexity of integrating AI into existing IoT ecosystems.

### 8.4.1 Data Privacy Concerns

AI systems require large amounts of data to function effectively, which can raise significant privacy concerns, particularly when dealing with sensitive information generated by IoT devices. To address these concerns, organizations must implement strict data governance policies, anonymize data where possible, and ensure compliance with privacy regulations such as the General Data Protection Regulation (GDPR) and the California Consumer Privacy Act (CCPA). By prioritizing data privacy and security, organizations can build trust with users and stakeholders, ensuring that AI-driven IoT security measures do not compromise individual rights.

## 8.5 Learning?

The intersection of AI and IoT security offers tremendous potential to address the unique challenges posed by connected devices. By leveraging AI's capabilities in anomaly detection, predictive maintenance, automated response, and more, organizations can significantly enhance their IoT security posture. However, successful implementation requires careful planning, ongoing adaptation, and a commitment to addressing the challenges associated with AI deployment. As the IoT landscape continues to grow and evolve, AI will play an increasingly vital role in securing the connected world of tomorrow, ensuring that IoT technologies can be used safely and effectively to drive innovation and improve quality of life.

# 9

## Future Trends and Predictions

**CONTENTS**

| | | |
|---|---|---|
| 9.1 | Introduction and Basic Concepts | 59 |
| 9.2 | Quantum Computing and AI Security | 60 |
| | 9.2.1 Discussion Points | 60 |
| 9.3 | Preparing for AI-Enhanced Cyberattacks | 61 |
| | 9.3.1 Discussion Points | 61 |
| 9.4 | Discussion | 62 |
| 9.5 | Learnings? | 63 |

## 9.1 Introduction and Basic Concepts

In this paper, we turn our attention to the horizon of AI and ML in cybersecurity, exploring the emerging trends and future directions that are poised to shape the landscape of digital security. As we look ahead, it's clear that these technologies will continue to play a transformative role, driving new approaches and solutions to ever-evolving threats. This chapter is designed to help you anticipate these changes, providing insights into how AI and ML are expected to develop and what that means for your cybersecurity strategies.

We'll delve into key trends, such as the increasing integration of AI-driven automation in security operations, the rise of AI-enhanced threat intelligence, and the growing importance of real-time analytics powered by machine learning. We'll also consider the potential impacts of advancements like quantum computing, which could revolutionize cryptographic methods and redefine what's possible in both offensive and defensive cybersecurity strategies.

Additionally, this chapter will address the challenges that come with these innovations, including the need for more sophisticated defenses against AI-powered cyberattacks and the ongoing ethical considerations around AI deployment. By understanding these trends and their implications, you'll be better equipped to adapt your strategies, ensuring that your security measures are not only up-to-date but also forward-thinking and resilient.

The goal of this chapter is to prepare you for the future of AI in cybersecurity, empowering you to stay ahead of the curve as technologies and threats continue to evolve. By examining what lies on the horizon, you can ensure that your approach to digital security remains innovative, effective, and ready to meet the challenges of tomorrow. As we wrap up this journey, let this chapter serve as both a guide and a call to action—to not just keep pace with change but to lead with insight and adaptability in the dynamic world of cybersecurity.

## 9.2 Quantum Computing and AI Security

Quantum computing is on the verge of revolutionizing numerous fields, and its impact on AI and cybersecurity could be particularly profound. With its ability to process and analyze vast amounts of data at speeds far beyond the capabilities of classical computers, quantum computing promises to both strengthen security measures and introduce new challenges. As we stand on the brink of this technological leap, it's essential to understand how quantum computing could reshape the landscape of digital security.

### 9.2.1 Discussion Points

One of the most exciting prospects of quantum computing in cybersecurity is its potential to vastly improve encryption methods and intrusion detection systems. Quantum computers can solve complex problems that are currently infeasible for classical machines, enabling the development of new, more secure cryptographic algorithms. Imagine encryption techniques that are virtually unbreakable, or intrusion detection systems that can analyze patterns and anomalies with unparalleled accuracy and speed. Exploring these possibilities helps us envision a future where security defenses are not just reactive but proactively fortified against even the most sophisticated threats.

However, quantum computing also introduces significant vulnerabilities, particularly concerning current encryption standards. Many of the encryption techniques that secure our digital world today, such as RSA and ECC, could be rendered obsolete by the sheer processing power of quantum machines. This raises the question: How do we protect data in a world where quantum computers can easily break existing encryption methods? AI could play a crucial role in this area, helping to develop quantum-resistant algorithms and providing dynamic defenses that can adapt to new forms of cyber threats. Discussing these vulnerabilities and the potential solutions AI might offer is critical as we prepare for a future where quantum computing is a reality. This exploration of quantum computing's dual impact on AI and cybersecurity—both as a powerful tool for enhancing security and as a new source of risk—underscores the need for proactive adaptation. By delving into these discussion points, we can better anticipate the changes on the horizon and begin crafting strategies that not only leverage quantum advancements but also safeguard against the new vulnerabilities they may bring.

## 9.3 Preparing for AI-Enhanced Cyberattacks

As AI technologies continue to advance, cyber adversaries are also evolving, leveraging these powerful tools to develop more sophisticated and effective attack methods. The future of cybersecurity will increasingly be shaped by the need to defend against AI-enhanced threats, where malicious actors use AI to outsmart traditional security measures. To stay ahead, cybersecurity strategies must evolve to anticipate and counteract these AI-driven threats, ensuring robust defenses in an ever-changing digital battlefield.

### 9.3.1 Discussion Points

With AI becoming more accessible and powerful, we can expect a rise in AI-enhanced cyberattacks that are more difficult to detect and defend against. Imagine phishing attacks that use AI to craft highly personalized messages that convincingly mimic legitimate communications, making them far more effective at tricking recipients. Similarly, AI-driven malware could learn from its environment, adapting its behavior to avoid detection by traditional security systems. These threats could also include automated attacks that exploit vulnerabilities faster than human response teams can react, or AI models designed to predict and counter defensive measures.To combat these evolving threats, cybersecurity must adopt proactive defense strategies that leverage AI's strengths. This includes developing AI systems capable of continuous learning and adaptation, allowing them to stay one step ahead of AI-enhanced attacks. For instance, deploying AI-driven threat detection models that evolve by learning from new attack patterns can significantly enhance defensive capabilities. Additionally, integrating adaptive response mechanisms that automatically adjust to new threats in real-time can help neutralize attacks before they cause significant damage. Building a robust AI defense also involves incorporating predictive analytics to anticipate potential threats, enabling preemptive actions that can disrupt attack plans before they are fully executed.

By exploring these discussion points, we can better understand the nature of AI-enhanced cyber threats and the strategies needed to defend against them. As cyber adversaries become more sophisticated, it's essential that our defensive measures evolve accordingly, using AI not just as a tool for protection, but as a dynamic, adaptable force that can anticipate and counteract the next generation of cyberattacks. This proactive approach will be critical in maintaining security and resilience in the face of increasingly intelligent and aggressive threats.

## 9.4 Discussion

As we look ahead to the future of AI in cybersecurity, it's important to consider how your organization can not only adapt to emerging technologies but also position itself to thrive in a rapidly evolving digital landscape. Reflecting on these forward-looking questions can help you gauge where your organization stands and what steps you can take to stay ahead of the curve in AI-driven security.First, think about how your organization can leverage advancements in quantum computing to enhance its cybersecurity measures. Quantum computing holds the promise of revolutionizing encryption and data security, offering new ways to protect sensitive information with unprecedented strength. Consider what specific aspects of your current security strategy could benefit from quantum enhancements, such as using quantum algorithms for more robust encryption or employing quantum-powered analytics to detect and respond to threats faster. Reflect on how you can start integrating quantum-ready practices now, even before the technology becomes mainstream, to ensure a smooth transition as quantum computing capabilities expand.

Next, reflect on what steps your organization can take now to prepare for potential AI-enhanced cyber threats in the future. As cyber adversaries become more sophisticated with AI, it's crucial to start building defenses that can anticipate and counter these advanced attacks. This might involve investing in AI-driven security solutions that can continuously learn and adapt, training your teams to recognize AI-enhanced threats, and fostering a culture of proactive cybersecurity. Think about the tools, skills, and strategies you need to develop today to effectively defend against the AI-powered threats of tomorrow.

Finally, consider how your organization can contribute to and benefit from global efforts in AI cybersecurity governance. As AI continues to play a larger role in security, international collaboration and governance are essential to establishing standards and protocols that ensure the responsible use of AI technologies. Reflect on ways your organization can participate in these global discussions—whether through contributing to industry standards, collaborating with other organizations, or advocating for ethical AI practices. By engaging in these efforts, your organization can not only help shape the future of AI in cybersecurity but also stay aligned with the latest developments and best practices, positioning itself as a leader in the field.Engaging with these questions allows you to strategically plan for the future, ensuring that your organization is not only prepared for the challenges ahead but also actively shaping the evolving landscape of AI in cybersecurity. By leveraging new technologies, building robust defenses, and participating in global governance, you can help create a more secure and resilient digital world.

## 9.5 Learnings?

This chapter has offered a forward-looking perspective on the pivotal role that AI and ML will continue to play in cybersecurity, guiding us through the transformative impacts of emerging technologies like quantum computing, the evolving nature of AI-enhanced threats, and the importance of global collaboration. As we wrap up this chapter and the book, it's evident that the journey through AI and ML in cybersecurity is far from over. The field is dynamic and ever-evolving, demanding ongoing learning, adaptation, and a proactive approach to embracing new technologies and trends. Use the insights from this chapter as a springboard for your continued exploration and innovation in the exciting world of cybersecurity.

- Stay informed and adaptable to technological shifts like quantum computing that will reshape cybersecurity.

- Proactively develop defense strategies to counter advanced, AI-enhanced threats.

- Engage in global collaboration to strengthen cybersecurity through shared data and insights.

- Embrace continuous learning to keep pace with the rapid evolution of AI and ML in security.

- Leverage AI's potential to not only defend against but also anticipate and prevent future cyber threats.

# 10
## *Conclusion*

**CONTENTS**

| | | |
|---|---|---|
| 10.1 | Introduction | 65 |
| 10.2 | Key Takeaways | 66 |
| 10.3 | Future Challenges and Opportunities | 67 |
| 10.4 | Continuing Education and Resources | 67 |
| 10.5 | Discussion | 68 |
| 10.6 | Closing Thoughts | 69 |

## 10.1  Introduction

As we reach the conclusion of this enlightening journey through the complex world of AI and ML in security, the chapter serves as a culmination of the key insights and learnings we've gathered along the way. This final chapter not only encapsulates the comprehensive exploration we've undertaken but also sets the stage for your continued growth and development in this rapidly evolving field. It's a moment to reflect on the significant advancements in AI-driven security, the challenges that lie ahead, and the strategies we've discussed to navigate this dynamic landscape.

In this chapter, we'll revisit the major themes covered throughout the book, from understanding foundational AI concepts and integrating them into existing security frameworks, to tackling advanced topics like adversarial AI and quantum computing. By summarizing these learnings, we aim to reinforce the knowledge you've gained and highlight the practical applications that can be immediately applied to your security strategies.

Moreover, this chapter offers guidance on how to stay engaged with the ever-changing field of AI in security. The technologies, threats, and opportunities we've explored are constantly evolving, and maintaining a forward-looking perspective is crucial. We'll discuss ways to keep your skills and knowledge up to date, whether through ongoing education, participation in professional communities, or staying abreast of the latest research and developments in AI security.

As we draw this journey to a close, let this chapter serve as both a reflection on what you've learned and a roadmap for the future. Embrace the dynamic nature of security technologies, and continue to adapt, innovate, and lead in the pursuit of creating safer digital environments. The insights and strategies shared here are not the end but a foundation upon which you can build, grow, and make a lasting impact in the world of AI and ML in security.

## 10.2 Key Takeaways

Throughout this book, we have explored a wide array of topics, ranging from the foundational principles of AI and ML to their advanced applications in security. We've delved into ethical considerations, examined real-world case studies, and looked ahead to the future of technological advancements in this field. Here are some of the crucial takeaways that encapsulate the key insights from our journey:

AI and ML are not just buzzwords; they are transformative tools that are reshaping security strategies. Through advanced threat detection, predictive analytics, and automated responses, these technologies provide organizations with powerful capabilities to enhance their security infrastructures. By leveraging AI and ML, organizations can move beyond traditional, reactive approaches and adopt more proactive, adaptive security measures that better anticipate and mitigate potential threats.

However, the deployment of AI technologies comes with significant ethical and legal responsibilities. It's essential to strike a balance between harnessing the power of AI and upholding principles of privacy, transparency, and fairness. Ethical considerations and regulatory compliance are paramount to fostering trust in AI systems, ensuring that they are used responsibly and equitably. As these technologies continue to evolve, maintaining this balance will be critical to their acceptance and success.

Looking to the future, the security landscape will be increasingly shaped by emerging technologies like quantum computing and the growing sophistication of cyber threats. The rapid pace of these advancements calls for proactive strategies, including ongoing education, research, and international cooperation. Organizations must be prepared to adapt quickly, embracing new technologies while also developing robust defenses against evolving risks. By staying ahead of the curve and working collaboratively on a global scale, we can build a more secure digital future.

These key takeaways underscore the importance of not only understanding AI and ML in security but also actively engaging with the ethical, legal, and strategic dimensions of these technologies. As we continue to navigate this dynamic field, let these insights guide your efforts to leverage AI responsibly and effectively in the pursuit of enhanced digital security.

## 10.3 Future Challenges and Opportunities

As technology continues to evolve, the challenges and opportunities within security will grow alongside it, presenting both new risks and avenues for advancement:

security professionals must be ever-vigilant and forward-thinking as adversaries increasingly employ AI and ML to execute more sophisticated and stealthy attacks. The use of AI by malicious actors means that traditional defenses may no longer be sufficient, and staying ahead will require a commitment to continuous innovation and the adoption of advanced, adaptive security measures.

As we leverage AI to enhance security, it's crucial to address the ethical challenges that arise. The deployment of AI in security must be balanced with respect for individual rights and societal values, ensuring that these technologies do not infringe on privacy or fairness. Ethical considerations should be at the forefront of AI development, guiding the creation of systems that not only protect but also uphold the highest standards of integrity.

The pace of technological change, particularly the integration of AI with emerging fields like quantum computing, will demand ongoing education and adaptability from security professionals. Staying current with these advancements will be essential for effectively managing new types of threats and seizing opportunities to strengthen security infrastructures. Continuous learning and the ability to quickly adapt to technological shifts will be key to thriving in this fast-paced, ever-evolving field.

As we navigate the future of security, these elements will be crucial in shaping a resilient and proactive approach. By staying ahead of threats, committing to ethical AI practices, and embracing technological advancements, security professionals can better safeguard the digital landscape and drive the field forward in a positive direction.

## 10.4 Continuing Education and Resources

To stay relevant and effective in the ever-changing field of security, continuous learning is not just beneficial—it's essential. The rapid pace of technological advancements and the evolving nature of cyber threats mean that professionals must constantly update their knowledge and skills. Here are some key resources and avenues to support ongoing development in AI and security:

Professional Development Courses: Regularly engaging in courses and certifications can help you stay current with the latest AI and security technologies and best practices. Look for programs that focus on cutting-edge topics like machine learning applications, AI-driven threat detection, and advanced encryption techniques. Certifications from reputable organizations can not only enhance your skills but also demonstrate your commitment to professional growth and expertise in the field.

Industry Conferences and Seminars: Attending industry events is a great way to keep up with current trends and future predictions in AI and security. These gatherings offer the chance to network with peers, learn from leading experts, and gain insights into the latest tools and strategies being used across the industry. Whether it's a large conference or a more focused seminar, these events provide valuable opportunities to engage with the community and stay informed about the direction of the field.

Academic and Industry Research: Staying updated with the latest research publications, white papers, and case studies is crucial for understanding new threats and the evolving applications of AI in security. Regularly reading academic journals, industry reports, and research findings can provide deep insights into emerging technologies and innovative approaches to security challenges. This knowledge not only informs your current practices but also inspires new ideas and strategies for protecting against future threats.

By actively participating in these continuing education opportunities, you can maintain a strong foundation in the latest developments and ensure that your security strategies remain effective and up-to-date. Continuous learning empowers you to adapt to new challenges, embrace technological innovations, and contribute meaningfully to the advancement of security in a rapidly evolving digital world.

## 10.5 Discussion

As we conclude this journey through the transformative world of AI and ML in security, it's time to reflect on how you can integrate these concepts into your personal or organizational cybersecurity strategy. Consider the following questions to guide your next steps, ensuring that the insights gained from this book are actively applied to enhance your approach to digital security.

First, think about how you will apply the key learnings from this book to enhance your organization's security posture. Reflect on the specific strategies and technologies discussed—such as predictive security models, AI-driven threat detection, or ethical considerations—that are most relevant to your current security challenges. How can you incorporate these learnings into your existing frameworks to create a more robust, proactive, and adaptive security environment? Consider developing a plan that prioritizes the implementation of these advanced technologies in a way that aligns with your organization's goals and needs.

Next, consider what steps you will take to ensure you remain updated on the latest developments in AI and security. With the rapid pace of technological change, staying informed is crucial. Will you commit to ongoing professional development through courses and certifications, attend industry conferences, or regularly review the latest research and publications? Reflect on how you can build a routine that keeps you engaged with new trends and innovations, helping you maintain a competitive edge and adapt to emerging threats effectively.

Finally, think about how you can contribute to the ethical deployment of AI in security within your community or organization. Whether you're in a leadership position, part of a team, or even just starting out, everyone has a role to play in promoting responsible AI practices. Consider how you can advocate for transparency, fairness, and accountability in AI-driven security measures. This might involve developing guidelines, participating in discussions on ethical AI, or leading initiatives that prioritize responsible AI use. Reflect on the impact you can make by championing ethical considerations, ensuring that the deployment of AI in security not only protects but also respects the rights and values of individuals and society.

By reflecting on these questions, you can create a clear path forward that leverages the knowledge and insights gained from this book. Your commitment to continuous learning, proactive adaptation, and ethical responsibility will not only strengthen your security strategy but also contribute to the broader goal of building a safer, more secure digital world.

## 10.6 Closing Thoughts

This book has aimed not only to educate but also to inspire. As you close this final chapter, remember that the field of AI and ML in security is one of perpetual growth and transformation. The journey does not end here. Each day offers new opportunities to apply the knowledge you've gained, to face and overcome challenges, and to innovate for a safer digital world. Let the end of this book mark the beginning of your continued exploration and leadership in AI-driven security. Embrace the future with confidence and curiosity, armed with the insights and understandings you've acquired here.